THE WRITER'S PATH

The Writer's Path

*A Guidebook for
Your Creative Journey*

EXERCISES, ESSAYS, AND EXAMPLES

Todd Walton and Mindy Toomay

Ten Speed Press
Berkeley • Toronto

Ten Speed Press
P.O. Box 7123
Berkeley, California 94707
www.tenspeed.com

Distributed in Australia by Simon and Schuster Australia, in Canada by Ten Speed Press Canada, in New Zealand by Southern Publishing Group, in South Africa by Real Books, in Southeast Asia by Berkeley Books, and in the United Kingdom and Europe by Airlift Books.

Cover Design by Catherine Jacobes
Interior Design by Tasha Hall
Interior Photography by Todd Walton
Project Editor: Dave Peattie, BookMatters

The lines from "now all the fingers of this tree(darling)have" on page 23 © 1949, ©1977, 1991 by the trustees for the E. E. Cummings Trust, excerpted from *Complete Poems: 1904–1962* by E. E. Cummings, edited by George J. Firmage. © 1979 by George James Firmage. Used by permission of Liverwright Publishing Corporation.

"Short Poem" from *The Essential Rumi* on page 66 was originally pubished by Threshold Book. Reprinted with permission.

Excerpt from "Christopher Robin Gives Pooh a Party and We Say Good-bye" on page 97 from *Winnie-the-Pooh* by A. A. Milne, illustrated by E. H. Shepard, © 1926 by E. P. Dutton; copyright renewed 1954 by A. A. Milne. Used by permission of Dutton Children's Books, a division of Penguin Putnam Inc.

Library of Congress Cataloging-in-Publication Data
    Walton, Todd.
        The writer's path : a guidebook for your creative journey : exercises, examples, and essays / Todd Walton & Mindy Toomay.
          p.   cm.
        Includes index.
        ISBN 1-58008-160-6
       1. English language—Rhetoric—Problems, exercises, etc. 2. Creative writing—Problems, exercises, etc. I. Toomay, Mindy, 1951– II. Title.
       PE1413.W333   2000
       808'.042 21-dc21

                                        99-045409

First printing, 2000
Printed in Canada

1 2 3 4 5 6 7 8 9 10 — 03 02 01 00

For friends and family and fellow writers—all of you.

Contents

Todd's Preface

When I made my debut as a writing teacher, I had published four novels, dozens of short stories and essays, and several poems. I'd been paid to write screenplays, and my first novel had been made into a motion picture. I had no college degree, I had never taken a writing course, I had never read a book about the writing process, and I wasn't convinced creative writing could be taught.

Twelve years later, having worked with hundreds of writers of all ages and levels of experience, I am still not convinced creative writing can be taught. I *am* convinced that each of us is endowed with our own kind of verbal genius and that this genius can be encouraged.

When I began to teach, I discovered almost immediately that criticism, judgment, and analysis—however well-intentioned—have a crippling effect on all but the most self-confident writers. I became determined to invent, test, and refine exercises through which writers could explore various aspects of the writing process without fear of being judged or compared.

For a decade, I've been privileged to work with many groups and individuals, creating exercises in response to their various needs and interests. The exercises contained in this volume are the cream of the crop. I wish to thank the many teachers and writers who have urged me to compile these exercises in book form. Your persistence has been a blessing.

I could not have made this book without the guidance and contributions of my writing partner, Mindy Toomay, who will have the final word in this preface.

This book is steeped in our intention to inspire and encourage you as you write your way along the path. ॐ TW

Mindy's Preface

*"A writer is simply someone who engages
in the act (and art) of writing."*

I penned this definition in a journal long ago to remind myself that I was already a writer, that I didn't need anyone's recognition or approval to begin living the writing life. Up to that point, most of my livelihood had come from a myriad of un-writerly jobs, but through it all I had written down my thoughts and feelings, my dreams and wild ideas, my insights and reflections. And so, long before any of my articles or poems or books found their way into print, I considered myself a writer and was deeply nourished by the writing process.

Academic degrees and publication credits are fine achievements, but they are not essential to walking the writer's path. You will gain tremendous enjoyment and insight from working with words in a focused way, whether you keep your work private, share it with only your closest friends, or offer it to the world.

This book, then, is about process, not product; about practice, not perfection. We offer *The Writer's Path* to guide and ease your journey as a writer, whatever your past inhibitions, present level of experience, or future goals. If you long to write, the exercises here can help you tap into your creativity and develop your skill. If you are already a writer, they can enliven and enrich your work.

Crafting this book with my good buddy and writing companion, Todd Walton, has been a great joy. We hope the spirit of our friendship comes through in these pages, to support and cheer you along the way. ∽MT

Using This Book

Our book is divided into eight chapters, each containing exercises designed to awaken and stretch your various writing muscles. Some of these exercises take a few minutes to do; others take much longer. All are intended to unleash your writing flow and illuminate different aspects of the writing process.

You can start with the first exercise and work straight through to the end of the book, or skip around and sample exercises at random. We have designed this guide and crafted the exercise descriptions so that you can choose either approach. Reading the chapter introductions will give you a sense of how the book is organized and a feeling for where you might wish to start.

Each basic exercise provides step-by-step directions. We also describe variations and offer suggestions for using the exercise in your particular writing configuration: solo, partner, or group.

Scattered among the exercises are short essays that offer our personal reflections on the practice of writing.

The Examples
The first six chapters conclude with examples generated by the authors using exercises in that chapter. When you have selected an exercise to work with, you may refer to our examples to see how the process looks on paper, or feel free to proceed without consulting the examples. Some writers find examples illuminating; others prefer not to be influenced by them. We have grouped the examples at the end of each chapter, rather than embedding them within each exercise, to give you this option.

Not every exercise has a corresponding example. On the other hand, we have included multiple examples for some exercises to demonstrate the myriad possibilities of a single process.

We hope our examples will entertain you as well as clarify the exercises.

Free-writing

In many exercises throughout this book, you will be invited to practice "free-writing." What does this mean? In purely physical terms, "free-writing" is a matter of putting pen to paper and allowing yourself to write whatever wants to be written. In emotional terms, free-writing invites you to express your uninhibited feelings—all parts welcome, no word judged wrong or inappropriate. When we free-write we do it for ourselves. No one else need ever read or hear what we've written unless we choose to share it. This privacy is fundamental to the liberating nature of free-writing.

Some of us take to free-writing like happy puppies let off their leashes. Others feel anxious, even paralyzed, at the prospect of such liberation. Many timid writers have been programmed in school and at work to associate writing with drudgery and shame—something we *have* to do that will be harshly criticized. Free-writing can help us leap over the creative roadblocks born of such experiences. The more we free-write, the further we move beyond the painful constraints of trying to please our parents, teachers, or bosses.

Here are a few suggestions to help you with your free-writing.

- Free-writing is sometimes easier to do away from a desk, in a setting you associate with comfort and pleasure—a favorite sofa, the kitchen table, bed, or a beloved outdoor spot.

- Reading a poem or an evocative prose passage can be an inspiring way to start a session of free-writing. In our writing groups, we sometimes ask one of the writers to read us a favorite poem, and then we'll free-write for ten or fifteen minutes, ignited by the ideas and energy of the poem.

- Music can be a wonderful stimulant to free-writing (though some writers find it distracting). Experiment by trying out different musical recordings—at different volumes—either as background music for your writing or as a prelude to an otherwise silent free-writing session. Instrumental music tends to be less distracting than vocal music.

- The letter form can be a great way to free-write (see "Letter Forms," page 43). Imagine you're writing to someone you enjoy communicating with, and see how that affects your writing flow.

- Though it may seem antithetical to the notion of *free-writing*, designating a certain period of time for the process can make the session more effective. Experiment with the effect of time limits on your writing until you find a span of minutes that seems optimal for you. We have found that ten-minute spans of free-writing, particularly with a partner or in a group, work well in conjunction with more structured writing processes. Even five minutes of free-writing can be deeply satisfying.

- Free-writing is a good way to generate passages of prose and poetry to use in a number of the exercises you'll encounter throughout this book.

The more we free-write, the more *all* our writing embodies the emotional and creative freedom we gain from the practice.

Jump Starts

*I might write four lines
or I might write twenty.
I subtract and I add
until I really hit some-
thing I want to do.
You don't always whittle
down, sometimes you
whittle up.*

—Grace Paley

There is a widespread belief that a writer is supposed to struggle to create something out of nothing. If you share this belief, then getting started *will* be a struggle. But when you visualize your writing process as a sure-fire way to access a rich and ceaseless flow of thoughts, memories, images, and feelings, you need only begin and the words will follow.

The exercises in this chapter are designed to quickly involve you in the act of writing. These processes do not focus on end results. Though you *might* end up with something you love—a line or two, the start of a story, a surprising phrase— it's just as likely you'll end up with gibberish. In either case, your writing muscles will be stretched, and *that's* the point of Jump Starts.

These exercises are intended primarily for solo writing, though we've offered a few variations for partners and groups. If you'd like to try those variations, and you have never done interactive work, you'll want to read our chapter on Interactive Writing (page 23).

MAKING LISTS

Making a list is a form of shorthand free-writing, a wonderful way to release an abundance of ideas onto the page with no concern for proper grammar or logic. Be spontaneous. If something comes up that doesn't "make sense," write it down anyway.

Here is a list of possible list topics.

- Wild Animals

- Trees

- Favorite Foods

- Exotic Cities

- Books I Want to Read

- Important People in My Life

- Fantasies

- Regrets

- Things I Learned from My Mother (or Father)

- Lists I Want to Make

Basic Exercise

1. Choose one of the suggested list topics. Write this topic at the top of a blank page.

2. Write the numbers 1 through 10 down the left-hand side of the page.

3. Quickly write down the first ten items that pop into your head.

VARIATION 1. Make up your own list topic.

VARIATION 2. Choose a topic from a list you've made, and make it the title for another list.

		A List
1. Grown-ups	16. Politicians	*of*
2. Teenagers	17. Environmentalists	
3. Teachers	18. Literary agents	*People*
4. Poets	19. Lawyers	
5. Prisoners	20. Doctors	*Who*
6. Grandparents	21. Mystics	
7. Accountants	22. Buddhists	*Will Use*
8. Moms and dads	23. Christians	
9. Children	24. Moslems	*This*
10. Piano players	25. Unitarians	
11. Wrestlers	26. Bicyclists	*Book*
12. Movie stars	27. Frisbee players	
13. Novelists	28. Friends	
14. Explorers	29. Romans	
15. Therapists	30. Everyone!	

SENTENCE BEGINNINGS

Sometimes it's easier to start writing if we don't have to *think* about how to begin. With this exercise, the start has already been made; you need only jump into the flow.

1. Here are three sentence beginnings. On a blank sheet of paper, copy each beginning twice.

He opened the

She walked into

The children discovered a

> *Basic Exercise*
> (example on page 13)

2. Quickly complete all six sentences and read them aloud.

3. Here are three more sentence beginnings. Again, copy each one twice, then quickly complete all six sentences.

   What if I said to you

   You have nothing to do with

   We aren't sure if

   Read aloud.

4. Here are three slightly more abstract beginnings. Copy each beginning twice, then complete them.

   A man

   A woman

   The large

   Read aloud.

VARIATION 1. If you find yourself really enjoying completing a particular beginning or set of beginnings, keep using them until you run out of gas.

VARIATION 2. Write the first few words of a sentence, skip a line or two, write the first few words of another sentence, and so on until you have a list of nine beginnings. Use these beginnings (in groups of three) to repeat the Sentence Beginnings exercise.

VARIATION 3. Flip through the pages of a newspaper or favorite book and copy down the beginnings of nine sentences. Use these fragments (in groups of three) to repeat the exercise.

For Partners:

1. Take turns suggesting possible sentence beginnings. Choose three, then use them to complete the exercise. (Example on page 13.)

2. If you both really like a sentence one of you has written, make it the opening line of an exchange story. (See "Partner Writing," page 25.)

For Groups: Each person suggests the beginning of one sentence. Everyone in the group uses these beginnings to do the exercise.

WORD ACCUMULATION

It is liberating to practice writing without *thinking* too much. This exercise invites us to write without getting bogged down in rational decision-making. It is easier to *do* than to describe. You may find it useful to look at the examples before beginning.

1. Quickly write a single line about whatever pops into your head. This does not have to be a complete sentence. Write quickly. Try not to edit or censor yourself. Read aloud.

Basic Exercise
(examples on pages 14–15)

2. Choose **two** words from this line, and write two new lines containing those **two** words anywhere in the new lines. Different forms of the same word are acceptable (for example, "happen" might become "happening," "big" might become "bigger," and so on). Read aloud.

3. Choose **two** words from each of these two lines, and write four new lines containing the **four** words anywhere in the new lines. Read aloud.

4. Choose **two** words from each of these four lines, and create **eight** new lines containing the eight words anywhere in the new lines. Read aloud.

VARIATION 1. Begin the exercise with a "found" line, something from a poem or a story, a headline or billboard.

VARIATION 2. When you have your final eight lines, choose five of them and use them to do the Five-Line exercise on page 8.

A Sudden Transformation	A woman in one of our writing groups began a Jump Start exercise with a tirade about being mistreated by her boss. By the end of the process she'd created a tender poem about forgiveness, and was amazed at how her feelings toward her boss had shifted.⌇TW

FIVE-LINE EXERCISE

By doing this exercise quickly and playfully, we may short-circuit one of the biggest obstacles to creative outflow: the internal judge. This exercise can also help us develop a more positive attitude about rewriting. If the instructions seem confusing to you, consult the examples for clarification of the process.

Basic Exercise
(example on page 15)

1. Write five lines about whatever pops into your head. Write quickly, without editing. These need not be complete sentences or thoughts; single words and sentence fragments are fine.

2. Using some of the words from the first five lines, in any order, and adding a few new words if you need them, craft three new lines, leaving a blank line after each line.

3. On the lines you've left blank, write new second, fourth, and sixth lines that go with the existing lines.

4. Quickly cross out two words in each line. Don't worry about making the wrong choices.

5. Rework these lines so they sound pleasing to you. Be sure you end up with six lines of any length.

6. Cross out four entire lines.

7. Rewrite the two remaining lines so they sound pleasing to you, and leave a blank line between them.

8. Write a new second line that fits with the existing lines.

9. Cross out all but a total of five words.

10. Instinctively and quickly choose one word.

11. Write this one word at the top of a new page. This is the title for a short poem or burst of prose. Quickly write the piece.

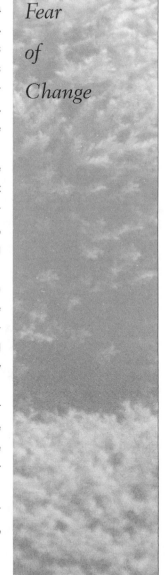

Fear

of

Change

I wrote a story in the seventh grade about a man who does battle with a giant octopus. I read it to my friends before turning it in to my teacher. They loved it and had me read it to them over and over again. A few days later, my story came back to me with a big "C −" above the title. My lines were slashed with red ink, and the margins were filled with critical comments. The words *Wrong* and *No* appeared several times on every page. At the end of the story my teacher wrote *Please Rewrite.* In tears, I tore the story to shreds.

To a greater or lesser degree, most of us have experienced the well-meaning criticism of our teachers as a rejection of our heartfelt creations. No wonder so many of us resist rewriting our poems or stories. We associate honing our creations with someone telling us, "No, you're doing it wrong," which most of us interpret as "Something is wrong with *you*."

When I began leading creative writing classes for teenagers, I ran into fierce antipathy to rewriting. The mere suggestion that they make changes to their initial drafts caused many of the students to stop showing me their work. Clearly, most of them had been severely traumatized by having their creations chopped up by teachers who didn't know any better.

Yet if my students wouldn't voluntarily rewrite, how could they ever experience the *craft* of writing? It was at this point that I began to devise exercises—as opposed to assignments—that allow writers to experience the mechanics of rewriting without being burdened with judgment or grades.

Once we experience rewriting as a way to make our work more powerful, the practice becomes a meaningful part of the writing process, rather than a punishment.⌇TW

Using the Dictionary

The dictionary is a marvelous tool for writers. We recommend that you consult one not only to check the spelling or definition of a word, but also to explore its multiple meanings and uses.

Here are two exercises, with variations, to help you deepen your relationship with your dictionary.

The Random Word

Basic Exercise (example on page 17)

1. Open your dictionary at random.

2. Without looking, bring the tip of your finger down on the page.

3. Read all the definitions of the word your finger landed on. If there are any unfamiliar words in these definitions, look them up, too.

4. Begin a session of free-writing (see page xiv) with a sentence containing the word you chose.

VARIATION 1. Use the word as the title of a poem.
VARIATION 2. Look up seven words in this random way, and use them all in a letter to a friend.

Exploring Words We Already Know

Basic Exercise (example on page 18)

1. Using a poem or prose piece you've already completed, or after generating work through a writing exercise, select a word that is essential to the meaning of your piece.

2. No matter how simple this key word is, look it up in your dictionary.

3. Read about the origins of your key word.

4. Look for something about the word you didn't already know.

When I was in high school, I had a delightfully eccentric English teacher named Mr. Nail. Once a week, he would read aloud to us from one of several dictionaries he kept stacked on his desk. He recommended we make it a daily practice to read a page or two from our dictionaries. He also informed us that dictionaries of the English language varied widely and that it would be worthwhile for us to eventually own at least two different ones. I don't read the dictionary every day, but whenever I look up a word (which I do frequently), I almost always read the definitions of a few other words on the page. ᧿TW

The Inimitable Mr. Nail

5. Write something—a poem or prose passage—about your key word.

6. Read your original poem or prose passage again, now that you've explored your key word.

VARIATION 1. Look up two or more key words from your poem or prose piece. Repeat the basic exercise for each word you've chosen to explore.

DOODLES AND SKETCHES

To doodle is to draw without anything in mind, simply letting the pen go where it wants to go. You may draw a picture, a pattern of lines, or a few random squiggles. It doesn't matter what you draw. The idea is to begin your writing by moving your pen on paper in a way that pleases and relaxes you.

Words from Doodles

1. Begin doodling at the top of your page.

2. After a minute or so, let your doodling become writing. Write for a few minutes.

3. Allow your writing to become doodling again. Doodle for another minute or so, thinking about what you just wrote.

4. Allow your doodling to become writing again.

Basic Exercise
(example on page 19)

A Novel Idea

One day, I made a series of unrelated little sketches on the same page. I remember one was of a man's face, one was of a wave, and one was of a hand holding a cigarette. A few days later, I wrote story ideas that sprang to mind as I looked at the images. Over the course of the next few weeks, I began making more little drawings to which I would append story ideas that sprang from the same creative impulse as the drawings.

One of the drawings, and the words it inspired, eventually evolved into my novel, *Ruby & Spear.* ᎙TW

VARIATION 1. Begin each interval of doodling at the top of a new page. This creates the effect of illustrated sections for your creation, whatever it turns out to be.

VARIATION 2. Before you begin to doodle, tell yourself you want a poem to emerge from the doodling.

For Partners: Using the technique described in "Partner Writing" (page 25), trade pages after each step of the Basic Exercise. In this way, you will be writing from each other's doodles. To mix your writing *and* your doodles, trade pages after each two steps of the basic exercise.

For Groups: Using the technique described in "Circle Writing" (page 28), pass your pages after each step of the basic exercise.

A Word from a Picture

Basic Exercise
(example on page 20)

1. Draw a picture of something—a flower, a box, a face—anything. The picture doesn't have to be more than a quick sketch, unless you want it to be.

2. Somewhere on the same page, write a single word that occurs to you when you look at the picture.

3. Use this word in a complete sentence.

4. Use this sentence as the beginning of a free-writing session (see "Free-writing," page xiv).

VARIATION 1. On the same page, write for a few minutes about whatever comes to mind when you look at your drawing.

Sentence Beginnings—*Basic Exercise, page 5 (TW/MT)*

He opened the meeting with a joke about frogs.
He opened the refrigerator without much hope.

She walked into her closet, thinking she was going out the front door.
She walked into his life without an itinerary.

The children discovered a new way of complaining.
The children discovered a hole in the fence large enough to wriggle through.

What if I said to you that time *isn't* money?
What if I said to you, "Bizragibble?"

You have nothing to do with the price of onions in Tokyo.
You have nothing to do with Myra's childhood.

We aren't sure if anyone really knows anything.
We aren't sure if another cup of coffee will make any difference.

A man was seen lurking near the aquarium.
A man emerged from the trees, a skinny stick balanced on his nose.

A woman gave me all my best ideas.
A woman with her thumbs tied sings.

The large chocolate bar hurled itself into her grocery cart.
The large loomed less large in the shadow of the colossal.

Sentence Beginnings—*Basic Exercise, Partner Writing, page 6 (TW/MT)*

On Tuesday morning, Reverend Meeks realized he was angry.
On Tuesday morning, the fog remained defiant.

Burnt Toast is my favorite Afro-Cuban band.
Burnt toast was the metaphor for my marriage.

Seventeen minutes after three, and still no sign of Harry.
Seventeen minutes of kissing you is all I can stand without screaming.

Word Accumulation—*Basic Exercise, page 7, Example 1 (TW)*

1. Write a sentence.

    I keep wanting to know what's going to happen.

2. Write two new lines containing two chosen words.

    He wondered how it **happened.** He had been
    wanting her to call him, and she had.

3. Write four new lines containing four chosen words.

    How do you get from here to there?
    First, figure out where you've **been.**
    Next, **call** in your spirit guide.
    Finally, ask what he or **she** thinks you should do.

4. Write eight new lines containing eight chosen words.

    "Get out of **here!"** screamed Harold. "I'm trying
    to **figure** out the exact dimensions,
    and **you've** been harassing me all morning.
    My **spirit** can't take it any more. **Next**
    you'll want me to give up carpentry and
    go back to selling aluminum siding."
    He bowed his head, took a deep breath,
    and said, "I'm sorry. **Do** whatever you want."

Word Accumulation—*Basic Exercise, page 7, Example 2 (MT)*

1. Write a sentence.

    Yesterday I planted the strawberry beds.

2. Write two new lines containing two chosen words.

    Yesterday I chose to not make the **beds**
    and spent all morning dancing instead.

3. Write four new lines containing four chosen words.

It was ***morning.*** Larry and June
sat down to ***make*** their decision. ***Instead***
of sticking around town to work all summer,
why ***not*** take off for Ireland?

4. Write eight new lines containing eight chosen words.

Their ***morning*** ritual was to head down to a café
upon awakening. ***Sticking*** around Deborah's
house tended to piss Pete ***off.*** It wasn't
working out, this roommate deal, and Sandra
knew it. They ***sat*** huddled in a corner of
Higher Grounds gulping ***their*** lattés, neither
one willing to mention the future. Suddenly
Sandra blurted, "I'd be happier in ***Ireland!***"

Five-Line Exercise—*Basic Exercise, page 8 (MT)*

1. Write five lines

I am traveling north for the sake of love.
Don't you dream of healing each other?
Whatever happens, keep your heart open.
For goodness and light, we sacrifice.
Make me a tuna sandwich, please.

2. Craft three new lines, using some words from first five lines.

Don't you dream of making light
traveling together, healing? For
goodness sake, whatever happens. Please.

3. Write new second, fourth, and sixth lines to go with existing lines.

Don't you dream of making light
work of this whole relationship thing,
traveling together, healing? For
once in your life, do something right for
goodness' sake, whatever happens. Please
don't blow this bléssed chance.

4. Cross out two words in each line.

~~Don't you~~ dream of making light
work of this ~~whole relationship thing,~~
traveling together, ~~healing?~~ For
once in your life, do something ~~right for~~
~~goodness' sake,~~ whatever happens. Please
don't ~~blow~~ this blessèd ~~chance.~~

5. Rework lines, ending up with six lines.

In my dream of making light
work of this relationship,
we travel together in
this life, loving
no matter what happens. Please,
accept this blessing.

6. Cross out four entire lines.

~~In my dream of making light~~
~~work of this relationship,~~
~~we travel together in~~
~~this life, healing~~
no matter what happens. Please,
accept this blessing.

7. Rewrite remaining two lines.

What happens when we accept
this blessing?

8. Write a new second line between existing lines.

What happens when we accept
ourselves and see our lives as
this blessing?

9. Cross out all but five words; read aloud.

~~What happens when we~~ accept
~~ourselves and see~~ our lives as
~~this~~ blessing?

[Read: "Accept our lives as blessing."]

10. Select one word.

   Accept

11. Use this word as the title of a short poem or prose piece.

ACCEPT

When love begins

to offer blessings,

open to life,

accept.

Dictionary Exercises—*The Random Word, Basic Exercise,*
page 10 (MT)

lasso *n, pl* **-sos** or **-soes.** A long rope or leather thong with a running noose at one end used especially to catch horses and cattle; lariat — *tr. v.* **lassoed, -soing, -sos** or **-soes.** To catch with or as if with a lasso; to rope. [Spanish *lazo,* from Latin *laqueus,* snare. See **lace.**]

Donna Mae felt rounded up, *lassoed,* and hog-tied in the presence of a tall, handsome stranger who had just lowered himself, slowly, onto a stool at the counter. Most of the customers at the coffee shop on any particular morning were regulars, as familiar and therefore uninteresting to her as frogs in the pond behind her parents' ranch house, where she'd spent practically her whole life.

She had approached the new man with order pad in hand, determined to take his unexpected appearance in stride, but she found herself standing mute before him, a bewildered look frozen on her face. Suddenly the words she had spoken at least a million times—"What'll ya have?"—struck her as improper and more than a little bit dangerous.

Examples

of

Jump

Start

Exercises

Dictionary Exercises—*Exploring Words We Already Know,*
Basic Exercise, page 10 (MT)

bewilder *tr.v* **-dered, -dering, -ders.** 1. to confuse or befuddle, especially
with numerous conflicting situations, objects, or statements. 2. *Rare.* To
cause to become lost —See Synonyms at **puzzle.** [BE- + archaic wilder, to
stray, probably from WILDERNESS.]

A MOMENT IN MUIR WOODS

Wandering lost
in a heaven of trees
we find each other, the fawn and I,
two stray animals, wide-eyed and wary,
shy in each other's company,
sensing we're close to comprehending
something tremendous,
yet not comprehending,
empty and free in the grace of not-knowing.
Blessedly bewildered.

Doodles and Sketches—*Words from Doodles, Basic Exercise, page 11 (TW)*

here's what I think. I need to stop blinking when the bullies get in my face. I want to stop listening to the nay sayers. You know what I mean?

I hear music in the wind. I see faces in the patterns in the dirt. I would love to go sailing and get somewhere where I could sleep in the sand and wake up to bagels and scrambled eggs.

Doodles and Sketches—*A Word from a Picture, Basic Exercise, page 12 (MT)*

KITCHEN

In the twilight, in the kitchen, Melody stirred something slowly with a wooden spoon, making perfect circles, silent and serious, as if entranced. Her mind was with the sensations: flesh of wood against the flesh of her fingers, soft wood against the hard metal pot, moist steam as it enveloped her face, a fragrant cloud. She thought of nothing beyond the kitchen walls as she chopped and poured and stirred. An artist in her studio, she gave herself totally to the work yet was magically filled in the process.

Soon Sonia would arrive, carrying Donnie in a backpack and two bottles of Merlot in her mittened fists. Cal would be late—he was helping his brother patch a fence—and he said he'd try to get Phyllis to come, too. His contribution to the feast would be a jar of Tupelo from the family hives, which would be spread on buttered cornbread to eat with Melody's chili.

Melody had washed two huge mounds of mustard greens, harvested that morning from the plot out back. She would steam them up with plenty of garlic, then splash them with olive oil and lemon juice and good soy sauce. Yams were in the oven, roasting in orange juice to intensify their sweetness.

The first real storm of autumn had inspired this feast—a gathering of old friends who brought humor and love and listening to the table along with the honey and wine, food for heart and spirit as well as body. They knew that together they could weather the coming winter. They would help each other survive.

I have worked with hundreds of writers—young and old—who have been baffled and bothered and shamed by stern admonitions, such as *"a writer should write every day for at least an hour."* This silly dogma—with a big, fat *should* at its heart—is like all dogma. It may work for some people, but not for everybody. In the case of writing, *shoulds* and *at leasts* work for almost no one, particularly when a person is in the early stages of establishing a writing practice.

When I am asked, "How many hours a day should a writer write?" I tend to reply along the lines of, "A writer should write for as long as she wants to write. If that's for five minutes on Tuesday and four hours on Friday, every other week, that's fine."

Here are some questions to ask yourself, and perhaps write about, as you establish or modify your writing practice.

- What time of day is most conducive to your word flow?

- Where do you like to do your writing?

- Do you feel uninhibited while you write?

- Have you found a pen you love the feel of?

- Do you prefer to write in a notebook or on loose pages?

- Is your writing time sacrosanct?

- Do you have a ritual for beginning your writing sessions?

- What do you enjoy most about writing?

- What beliefs do you hold about what a writer is *supposed* to do? Where did you get these ideas? Do they seem applicable to you?

- Why do you want to write?

- What are the most difficult parts of the writing process for you? How do you deal with them?

- Do you share your writing with others?

- Do you think of yourself as a particular kind of writer? A poet? A fiction writer? An essayist? A playwright? Is your self-definition satisfying?

- Can you find a way to make your writing a higher priority in your life?

- Do you set goals for yourself? Why?

- Who are you writing for? One other person? An imagined audience? A known audience? Yourself?

- Who are your favorite writers? How do you imagine they go about creating the works you admire?

- What do you enjoy more than writing? Why?

ॐTW

$\mathcal{I}$NTERACTIVE WRITING

and now you are and
 i am now and we're
a mystery which will
 never happen again,
a miracle which has
 never happened
 before—
 —e.e. cummings

Working with other writers is fun, challenging, inspiring, sometimes frustrating, but always worth a try. Every partnership or group will have its own personality and energy dynamics. Getting acquainted and learning to trust and respect each other will animate the early stages of interactive work and lay the foundation for a fruitful long-term collaboration. Once you and your partner or group have become adept at Partner or Circle Writing, Sketching, and Interviewing, every exercise in this book can be approached using those techniques. You may also find yourselves inventing unique variations suited to your own dyads and groups. For more on group writing, see chapter seven, "The Writing Group," page 201.

PARTNER WRITING

Combining energies with a writing partner—synergy—can provide the extra push you both need to get your writing juices flowing. Even if you don't have a regular writing companion, Partner Writing can be a fun and interesting way to engage with a friend or child.

Basic Exercise
(examples on pages 34–35)

1. Each of you write one line—whatever pops into your head. This need not be a complete sentence, but should span roughly the width of your page. Part of the fun and challenge of this exercise comes from completing each other's sentence beginnings. However, it's fine if the end of your line happens to be the end of a sentence.

2. Exchange pages (or notebooks) and read your partner's line to yourself, then quickly continue their train of thought for a second line.

3. Exchange pages again. Each of you silently read the two lines you've created together, and continue that train of thought for another line.

4. Continue exchanging pages and writing new lines eight more times for a total of ten exchanges.

5. On the last exchange, each of you may write a few extra lines to wrap up the prose piece or poem.

VARIATION 1. Repeat the exercise, this time writing two or three lines each before exchanging pages.

VARIATION 2. Repeat the exercise, this time writing a paragraph each before exchanging.

VARIATION 3. One of you suggest a word or phrase that must appear somewhere in the first line of each piece (for example, "golden" or "never again" or "she couldn't believe").

VARIATION 4. Agree on a general style before you begin. You might decide to write a fictional memoir in first person, a piece of descriptive prose in third person, a fairy tale, or a mystery.

For Solo Writers: If you want to try a version of this exercise, start different lines on two or three sheets of paper, then go back and forth from one story to another.

For Groups: Try pairing up different people each time the group does Partner Writing. Be sure to read your creations aloud to the group. It's fascinating and often very funny to hear what different dyads come up with.

Notes:

- For all interactive exercises, everyone involved should use the same size of paper. Working with more than one size (and therefore different line lengths) may make for interesting variations, but it may also disrupt a good back-and-forth pace.

- We know several writers who have found long-term writing partners by doing Partner Writing as members of a larger group. (See "Finding a Writing Partner" on page 27.)

Finding a Writing Partner

When my beloved seventh grade teacher, Mrs. Cushenberry, posted my poem entitled "Autumn Leaves" in the hallway outside our classroom, for a while I considered officially "becoming" a poet. I had no real idea what that might mean. The images that came to mind were of a rail-thin Edgar Allen Poe hunched over his pen in a freezing garret and of Emily Dickinson pouring her longing for love into poetry. I didn't feel drawn to such sad scenarios, so there and then I abandoned the notion of a career in poetry, deeming it too lonely.

It's true, of course, that a certain measure of solitude is required for writing. We need to be alone with our ideas and visions often and long enough to pin them down. Writing with others is an antidote to this necessary aloneness, and it can reinvigorate your work with playfulness and an expanded sense of creative possibility. Occasionally, the work you do with your partner will astound you with its brilliance. Always, you will be challenged and tickled by the experience of co-writing.

How does one find a writing partner? It may be as easy as asking around among friends and acquaintances. You may already know someone who shares your passion for writing and is eager for the support of joint practice. If nobody leaps at the suggestion, invite your friends over for a word-play party, using this book as a guide. Notice who contributes enthusiastically and imaginatively to the evening's activities, then make a date with them for a follow-up session.

Classes and workshops are logical places to meet other writers in your area, and a regular writing group can yield any number of wonderful candidates. You might also try frequenting libraries or cafés where artistic types congregate, staying on the lookout for a scribbler whose appearance and attitude you find appealing. Strike up a friendly conversation (or slip them a note), and see where it leads. You might even find a writing partner by running a "common interest" ad in the classified section of a community publication.

If you remain open to finding a writing partner, he or she will eventually appear. Meanwhile, continue your solo practice and seek out the company of other human beings for recreation and fellowship. Being committed to your writing practice doesn't have to feel like being banished from society.~MT

The Mystery of Melinda Todd

Melinda Todd is the real author of stories Mindy and Todd write together. She is more than just a name we invented. She is an actual being composed of...Well, here's what happened.

We were writing together one day in a café, a cold rain drumming on the pavement outside. We were passing pages back and forth over a pot of tea, taking turns finishing each other's sentences and losing ourselves in the fun and flurry of story-writing. We finished our stories at exactly the same moment and discovered when we read them aloud that we had both ended with the word "twins."

"You realize," said Mindy, tapping her pen on the table, "how often this sort of thing happens now?"

"Maybe we're becoming a single entity," Todd suggested, his eyebrow steeply arched.

A deep silence fell. We both needed a moment to contemplate the mystery of what had happened to us over the months of writing together—months of learning to let go of our need to control outcome, of learning to trust and believe in our separate/mutual artistry.

Even now, she is writing this memoir of her birthing. We don't know where she came from or where she's taking us, but we delight in recording her stories.↗Melinda Todd

CIRCLE WRITING

For Circle Writing you'll need a group—we have found five to seven people to be an ideal size—and plenty of loose sheets of paper. We recommend lined paper, unless *all* the members of your group are neat, level-handed writers. Without lines, things can get out-of-line (slanty) in a hurry. Everyone should make an effort to write legibly because one of the big payoffs of Circle Writing comes from hearing the group's creations read aloud. Having to stop reading in the middle of a story to interpret someone's scrawl is time-consuming and distracts from the free flow of the process.

Basic Exercise
(example on page 36)

1. Each of you write a first line. As in Partner Writing, this need not be a complete sentence, but should roughly span the width of the page.

2. When you have all completed your first lines, pass your pages to the left.

3. Read the line to yourself, then write a second line that seems to match the style of the first line.

4. When all of you have completed your second lines, pass your pages to the left again.

5. Continue this process until all the pages reach the people to the right of the people who began the pages.

6. Take turns reading the creations aloud.

Writing Sexy

A ten-session (once a week) writing workshop began promisingly. The usual first-session jitters gave way to a scintillating second session, everyone trusting more deeply that there would be no criticism, no comparison.

At the end of this second session, I introduced the group to Circle Writing, and we produced several satisfying stories. As it happened, *every* contribution by Fritz (not his real name) was overtly sexual in content. This caused considerable discomfort for three members of the group, each of whom complained to me in private the next day. I urged patience. I also decided not to do any Circle Writing for our third session. However, when several members eagerly suggested we finish that third session with Circle Writing, we did. Once again, Fritz turned every group story into something sexual, and the complaints about him doubled. I asked the unhappy writers to trust in the power of our writing together, and to have a little more patience.

For our fourth session we did nothing but Circle Writing. I stated again that the process was about giving ourselves to the group mind and allowing each line to spring from the previous one, not solely from our separate imaginations.

Midway through this session, Fritz began to write in harmony with the other writers. He had a penchant for writing about sex and sexual desire and, when it fit the tone of the piece, he almost always "wrote sexy." But when the story was not about sex, he gave himself fully to the established tone.

For our last session—more party than practice—Fritz's original detractors thanked him for opening them up to "writing sexy." ॐTW

Notes:

- Your group can, of course, pass the pages to the right rather than the left. Decide on the direction before you begin.
- If your group is small—three to five people—circulate the pages two or three times.
- If group members write at widely varied speeds, you may wish to assign one member—the happy medium—to say "Pass" when he or she finishes writing her line or lines. Since it's fine if someone stops writing in mid-sentence, this arbitrary "Pass" command can keep the pages from piling up behind the slowest writer in the group.

VARIATION 1. Repeat the exercise, writing two or three lines each before passing the pages.

VARIATION 2. Repeat the exercise, writing a paragraph each before passing the pages.

VARIATION 3. Decide on a word or phrase to appear somewhere in the first line of each person's piece.

VARIATION 4. Agree on a general style before you begin. You might decide to write a fable ending with a moral, a fictional confession, a period piece, or a narrative poem.

SKETCHING

We call this exercise Sketching because it is very much like the warm-up exercises employed by visual artists. Sketching helps us look more closely at things we might otherwise only glance at or not see at all. These details of life, and the ways in which they combine, add richness and color to our writing. This exercise should be done quickly. The less time we take, the more likely it is that our words will spring from what we see, not from what we think.

For this exercise, one writer serves as the "artist's model" for the other writers. If you're working with a group, each of you in turn should act as the model. If you're working as partners, take turns being the model. If you're working solo, use a mirror, or ask a friend to pose for you.

Basic Exercise
(example on page 38)

1. Have the model sit still. Look at the model. In the center of your first line, write the first word that comes to your mind.

2. Now look at the model again. Directly below the first word you wrote, write the next word that comes to mind. It is essential that your words come from what you see. Try not to succumb to word association. Look and write, look and write, creating a column of seven single words. Read the words aloud.

3. Now, referring to the model again, create a second column of words to the left of the first column. Again, it's important

for these words to come from looking at the model. Look and write, look and write. When you've completed this second column of seven words, read the two-word lines aloud.

4. Next, create a third column of words to the right of the first two columns. Look and write, look and write. Now read your three-word lines aloud.

5. If you want to do more with these lines, think of them as a rough draft. Perhaps you'll want to rework the words to create a poem or a descriptive prose piece. You may wish to apply some of the steps of the Five-Line Exercise (page 8) to what you generate by Sketching.

VARIATION 1. Create an assemblage of objects on a table. Do the Sketching exercise using this assemblage.

VARIATION 2. Choose a single object to "sketch." Experiment with different sizes and types of objects.

VARIATION 3: The model moves instead of holding still.

For Partners and Groups: There are countless things you can do with the three-word lines the group generates. Here are a few suggestions.

- After all the members of the group have modeled, each person uses the word-sketches the others have made of them to craft a poem or prose description of themselves.

- The model writes about her experience of modeling— how she felt during the process, what she imagined people were seeing, which words from the word-sketches about her were surprising, enlightening, alarming.

- After the Sketching exercise, free-write for five minutes.

Note: Sketching exercises lend themselves well to writing in cafés or libraries, where interesting people and objects abound.

(For a fascinating group variation on the basic exercise, see "Directed Sketching" on page 207.)

Writing What We See

When I was seventeen, I decided to institute daily self-disciplines to speed my process of becoming a writer. As part of my practice, I gave myself the task of describing what I saw. Sometimes I wrote about the objects and their arrangement on my desk. At other times, I wrote about what I saw out my window. I also took my notebook into the woods, or to a café, and wrote descriptions of what I observed. This practice helped me refine my descriptive powers and freed me from the habit of generating words exclusively from my memory or imagination.⨀TW

BASIC INTERVIEW PROCESS

The interview process is a great way to ignite memories, create characters, and develop story lines. *Asking* questions of ourselves and others helps focus our attention. *Answering* questions inspires us to investigate our thoughts and feelings more deeply.

Basic Exercise
(example on page 39)

1. Write a question on a blank piece of paper. Read the question aloud.

2. Write a thoughtful answer, as though you were responding to a reporter, talk-show host, or biographer.

3. Continue asking and answering until you've gone through a series of six questions.

VARIATION 1. Create a fictional self by inventing answers to the questions, rather than answering from your actual experience.

VARIATION 2. Answer half the questions from your actual experience, half from a fictional perspective.

VARIATION 3. Focus the interview by writing a title at the top of the page. Allow this title to suggest the questions.

For Partners: Each of you write a question. Exchange pages. Each of you write an answer to the other's question, then write a new question. Continue this process for as long as you like.

For Groups: One person in the group asks a question out loud. Everyone, including the questioner, writes an answer. The next person asks a question, and everyone writes an answer. Continue this process until everyone has asked a question. Now share your interviews aloud.

Some questions you might ask:

* What's your favorite movie? Why?

* What are your earliest food memories?

* How did you get from here to there?

* Tell us a little bit about your latest performance piece.

* Where have you been in the last year?

* Who was your favorite teacher? Why?

* Who are you still in touch with from the old days?

* What happened to your dog?

* What do you do on Wednesday nights?

* Why did you choose that line of work?

* Who gave you that black eye?

* Why Iceland?

* Where were you standing when it happened?

* What happened to you in the Army?

* Where did you find that stone?

* You're not exaggerating, are you?

* What's the meaning of your sculpture?

* Could you elaborate?

* How do you expect to earn a living doing that?

* How does one become a Buddhist?

* How does it feel to be adored by millions?

* How could you have done something like that?

Note: In our Character chapter we will remind you of how effective the interview process can be for developing the personalities and life stories of your characters (page 110). In our Story chapter we will demonstrate how the interview process can be used to create stories (page 166).

Partner Writing—*Variation 2, page 26 (TW/MT)*

One paragraph each before exchanging pages.

THE MIDDLE BRICK

It wasn't that the news itself was so terribly sad. Aunt Martha's mind had been lost to Alzheimer's for several years and lately her physical abilities had been waning rapidly, so her death was in some sense a relief, a blessing. But the call from his mother had hit Stanley very hard. He was weeping loudly at his kitchen table, remembering his boyhood and how permanent everything had seemed then.

A loud clonk broke into his weeping, and he looked up out the window expecting to see a fallen branch but instead found himself staring into the eyes of an old man, his wizened face inches from the window, wearing a wild expression. Stanley rose to his feet, frowning, confused out of his grieving by this sudden intruder. And what had made the clonking sound, he wondered? He wiped his eyes and went to the back door to see what this old man wanted and what, if anything, he'd broken.

Stanley opened the door only a few inches but before he could speak the man had reached in and gripped his arm urgently. Stanley gasped at the old geezer's strength. "Let go," he demanded. "What do you want?"

"I want that which doesn't exist," the old man said, flashing a toothless grin. "I come from the place beyond Nowhere."

"And where might that be?" asked Stanley, unable to maintain his anger in the face of such delightful absurdity.

"A good cup of coffee," said the old man. "Is that which doesn't exist. And I used to live here in this very house. Before they locked me up. My own children. After my stroke. But I got out." He blushed. "I broke your flowerpot. Sorry."

"I *have* coffee," said Stanley, thinking of Aunt Martha and how perversely hilarious it would have been to set her up with this old guy. "Good coffee."

"I thought you'd never ask," said the old man. "I'll be the judge of that."

Stanley opened the door wide, wiping his nose on the

sleeve of his sweatshirt. He smiled sheepishly at the man and waved him in.

"Snot's okay," the man said breezily. "No law against snot."

Stanley pulled out a chair for his guest to sit on, but the old guy walked slowly around the room. "I built this place," he finally said.

"Really?" said Stanley, bemused. "You're Alfred Whitely?"

"*The*," said the old man. "Come on. I'll show you something about this place nobody knows because it's a secret only I know."

Stanley followed Whitely into the living room where the old man knelt before the large brick fireplace. "Kneel beside me," he said.

Stanley did so.

"Look at the very middle brick."

"Which one is that?"

The old man pointed at it. Stanley looked at it.

"Now stare at it without blinking for as long as you can."

Stanley did so, and as he did he began to feel, well, euphoric and he had an image of his Aunt Martha's beautiful spirit light rising effortlessly into the sky.

"Wow," said Stanley, looking at the old man. "I feel terrific."

"Thanks," said the old man, putting a hand on Stanley's shoulder. "Thought of it myself."

Partner Writing—*Variations 1 and 3, combined, page 26 (TW/MT)*

Two lines each, "animal" in first two lines.

ANIMAL INSTINCT

Bartholomew did not believe in fate or karma or anything at all spiritual, but he trusted animal instinct, and \\ *his* animal told him not to go down Broadway. It was longer to go around, but better to take more time and reach \\ his destination in one piece.

He pulled on his sweatshirt hood and strode onto Park Boulevard, the street of big houses, almost \\ too quiet for

Bartholomew's liking. Broadway would be a wild jumble of sounds and light and people and cars and company, some of it \\ unsavory, but comforting somehow. This rich people's street was a bit dead and, yes, he admitted, spooky. Several of the homes were \\ completely dark, and for a moment he was tempted to go into one of them and fix himself a drink, Scotch rocks. \\

A sudden sound in this silent landscape diverted his attention. He tensed, expecting maybe a guard dog to charge him, but instead an old woman in bathrobe and slippers, flashlight in hand, appeared from behind a hedge to his left.

"Seen \\ an iguana around here?" she asked, and Bartholomew relaxed.

"How big?" he asked.

The woman laughed. "You mean you saw more than one?" \\

She aimed her light beam at his feet, then dragged it slowly up to his face. "You live around here?"

"Used to," he said. "Now \\ I live south of Broadway. I know the Jacksons."

She moved the beam back to the bushes. "I'll give you five dollars if you find \\ Iggy," she said. "He's all I've got."

This was a ludicrous comment from a woman who lived in the most affluent \\ section of the city, but Bartholomew knew how such a paradox could work, how all the tea in China might not *feel* like \\ enough, how a person could feel absolutely empty despite being surrounded by expensive stuff. "I'll find him, ma'am, if it takes me all night."

She handed him the flashlight. "Well, when you do, ring my doorbell. You and I will have a cup of coffee. Pie, too. I've got a story or two I feel like telling."

Circle Writing—*Combination of Variations 1 and 3, pages 28–29*

These two three-line Circle Writing stories were created simultaneously. The instruction was to include the word "lemon" somewhere in the first three lines. Our circle consisted of five writers: Bill Yates, Carolyn Schneider, Dave Peattie, TW, and MT. Slashes indicate places where story was passed to the next writer.

PABLO'S GROVE

I live a lemon life, kind of sour and also refreshing—not nutritious but zesty, and in a golden glow like sunrise or the yolk of a really fresh egg. That is the reason \\ I was attracted to the idea of purchasing a lemon grove. It was listed under "Business Opportunities" after the "Lazy R" dude ranch. \\ My Uncle raised walnuts; I could raise lemons, I thought. So I put everything I owned or could borrow down on the place, and hired \\ a sixty-year-old Mexican lemon expert to tend the trees. I didn't realize for quite a long time that Pablo knew a lot about many things, not just lemon trees. He had \\ a way with rain clouds and honey bees and he could sing songs to attract sympathetic birds whose songs made the branches reach with lovely urgency toward the clouds he \\ summoned with a hat dance. I was entranced, and re-read all of Carlos Castaneda, until one day I tossed the book over my shoulder and began humming, quietly at first, then \\ loudly, singing to the farthest corners of the grove. It was an aria of sorts, and I was joined by the aviary chorus and the buzz of insects. \\ A yellow light shone on the porch of the gods that day. Citrus groves undulated in lemony waves of music that was in my head and \\ I had to admit a certain sweetness had entered me. I actually called my ex-wife, Mildred, that evening and told her I had forgiven myself and hoped \\ she would find the strength to bake me one more lemon meringue pie before she dies (she's only 49). And she said the sweetest thing. She said, "Merl. Good on you. You're a peach."

WHAT SHE IS

My mom is a lemon. You can't really give 'em back, and it doesn't do much good to put signs out in front of her house \\ offering her for sale as a refreshing beverage. So I've learned to simply sit with her, without feeling the need to respond to her every \\ sneer and grunt. My mom is a princess. She didn't fit the glass slipper, so the prince she got, my dad, was no Rolls Royce. He was more of a Studebaker, built \\ so long ago that no new parts are available and the glove compartment drops open without warning and clangs on her ample knees, justifying her eye-rolling and \\ wincing. My mom is a locomotive. She can come barreling through your life and there is nothing you can do to stop her. No air brakes on her. \\ She is a train, made of parts that look about like any others—and when she's on a bus bench or sitting in church, or anywhere except \\ her astro-turfed patio, she seems kind of ordinary, or so people tell me. At home, she hauls out a list of complaints and regrets you wouldn't believe. Once \\ she told me, "Gerald, I have been unfair to you. You are not a bad son. You are inadequate as a human being. I heard a psychologist on television use that expression and \\ apparently this condition can be cured through drugs and a short but firm stay in a locked facility. Not that you're crazy—just a deep disappointment and a poor financial planner." \\ My mom is about all I've got, and I'm all she's got. I may be a disappointment but at least I am *her* disappointment. And she may be a carbuncle on the hind side of humanity, but she's *my* carbuncle and she lets me stay with her for $78 a month.

Sketching—*Basic Exercise, Variation 2, page 30 (TW)*

STILL LIFE

pupils	gray	fur
paws	white	shadow
sun	eyes	reflection
claws	hair	slope
whiskers	ears	drowse
dots	stripes	pattern
grin	mouth	light

Poem from sketching lists

LAP CAT

Her pupils—black slits in green

marbles embedded in gray velvet—

her white chest in shadow,

a patch of sun on her sloping flank

reflected in her eyes.

She grins and drowses,

her claws seeking purchase

through my thin shirt,

no thought for my possible pain,

for what comes next.

Basic Interview Process—*Basic Exercise, page 32, Partners (TW/MT)*

Initials are included to demonstrate the exchange process.

Where did you first feel at home? (TW)
Underneath a great maple tree that dominated Uncle Leo's backyard. This was in Poland still, before we fled. I must have been seven or so when I had my first experience of belonging to this earth. I felt this tree was my relative in a way no human being had ever been. (MT)

Before that you were unhappy? (MT)
Happy? Funny question. My friend, Sal, who is the most spiritual agnostic you can possibly imagine, says the pursuit of happiness is an addiction more destructive than an obsession with money, sex, anything. Why? Because true happiness is when you don't know what you're feeling. True? Who knows? Was I unhappy? Well, I was hungry and curious. What else? (TW)

Examples

of

Interactive

Writing

Exercises

Do you often think in questions? (TW)

You tease me, I know. But it is true that questions are more important to me than answers. And I find it helpful always to keep searching for the next question, the deeper exploration. Otherwise, life becomes static, no? (MT)

You have survived great deprivation in your lifetime. How has this shaped you? (MT)

I have come to believe I never suffered. Yesterday I was in terrible pain, or so I thought, because my cousin Lorraine completely forgot our lunch date and then made a curt little excuse that almost sounded like she was blaming me. I mean, I was in agony. *(Laughs.)* And in that moment, what was my time in Auschwitz? What is suffering? In every moment there are angels by the millions hovering. (TW)

So you believe in angels? (TW)

Absolutely. I don't pretend they look like the sculptures in the great cathedrals, but I feel them with me a great deal of the time. If this is just my imagination, as some would claim, then I say imagination is itself an angel, a protector and a guide and a helper. You see? (MT)

ℒETTER FORMS

*The sending of a letter
constitutes a magical
grasp upon the future.*
—IRIS MURDOCH

W hat's the difference between a story written for publication or for a teacher and a story written as a letter to a friend? Aside from the opening, "Dear Rico," there may be no *technical* difference whatsoever. But the difference in our sense of love and trust for the people who might see or hear our words is enormous.

Letters to friends are more relaxed, less rule-bound, and more conversational than most other forms of writing. We feel known and understood as we write to a friend, and this in itself can be verbally liberating. So if you find yourself struggling with any of the exercises in this book, recall the suggestion: *Try this exercise as a letter to your best friend.*

LETTERS

Here are four letter-writing exercises that have proved especially inspiring to the writers with whom we have worked.

So, there I was . . .

Basic Exercise	1. Write a letter to a friend in which you tell a story, fictional or actual. Keep your friend in mind as you write the story. 2. Read the letter. 3. Imagine sending this letter to someone other than the friend you wrote it to. Are there any parts of the story you would change, embellish, or delete? Write this modified letter, if you wish.

A Person I Know

Basic Exercise (example on page 54)	1. Write a letter to a friend describing an interesting person you know or a character you've imagined. Focus on those aspects of the person or character that you think your friend would be most interested in. 2. Reverse the process. Write a letter to the person or character you just described to your friend, telling them about your friend.

To

You

Dear Friend,

I enjoy writing letters to friends more than any other part of my writing practice. I'm sure much of my enjoyment comes from imagining my friends receiving and enjoying my letters.

I think of letter writing as a form of gift giving.

I also think of letter writing as instant publication. If I like my letter, it goes directly to my audience—a most satisfying feeling.

And though I love *getting* letters, I don't expect replies to my missives. Releasing expectation frees me from disappointment. Free of disappointment, I continue to write and send letters every day. The result of this unbridled writing and sending? Nearly every afternoon, a person in a pale blue uniform brings me handmade messages—cards and letters and stories and poems—from friends near and far.

Love, Todd

I've written a great many letters to my mother since her death in 1976 when I was twenty-four. This has been a way to examine and express intense feelings, to honor and heal the past, to simply keep in touch. As I write, she comes vividly into my mind and all kinds of memories surface. It is not always a joyful process, but it's one I highly recommend. Writing to a loved one who has died is a special kind of therapy, and a special kind of prayer. ✒ MT

Healing the Past

Letter to Mother

Write a letter to your mother. If your mother is no longer alive, this may be a particularly powerful writing experience. Use any or all of the following suggestions to inspire your process:

Basic Exercise
(example on page 55)

• Share a memory about something she said or did.

• Ask her a question you've always wanted to ask her. Then tell her what you imagine the answer to be.

• Tell her what you've been up to recently.

• Tell her something you've never told her before.

• Find something to include with the letter—a poem, a story, an article, a photo, a leaf, a feather—anything you think she might appreciate.

Time Capsule Letters

Write a letter to yourself. When you're finished, put it away somewhere out of easy reach. Choose a date several months from now, and make a note on your calendar: *Read Letter to Myself.* You may also wish to note the hiding place.

Basic Exercise

Here are some suggestions for what might go into the letter.

• Describe how you're feeling.

• Talk about what you hope to accomplish in the next few days or weeks.

- Describe something that recently happened to you.

- Make some predictions.

- Give yourself some advice.

- Write a spontaneous poem.

- Name the last book you read and the last movie you saw, and share your thoughts about them.

- Talk about the significant people in your life.

- Note three major events happening in the world.

A Vindication

I was asked to speak to a group of supporters of a local library. When I made my presentation, I told the group I had written them a letter—which I then read—because I often found it the best way to get my thoughts onto paper. Afterwards, a woman approached me and told me the following story: "I started writing letters almost as soon as I learned to write. We lived way out in the country in Nevada, so letter writing was my way of being connected to the outside world. I wrote to my grandmother in San Francisco, my cousins in Idaho, and I had three pen pals, one in Japan, one in Germany, and one in Texas. I loved to write letters because it meant I'd *get* letters! I went to a little country school, and I had the same wonderful teacher from first grade to sixth. She allowed me to write my essays and stories as letters, just so long as my grammar was good.

"Then I skipped two grades and went into ninth grade. When I wrote my first essay on Abraham Lincoln as a letter *to* Abraham Lincoln, my teacher gave me an F, and then she ridiculed me in front of the whole class. Now, I'm the kind of person who gets mad instead of depressed, so I set out to prove I was the best writer in the class, which I did. I still wrote all my rough drafts as letters and then translated them into essay form.

"I felt vindicated tonight to hear you say letters are a great way to write whatever you want to write. Makes me want to write a whole novel as a letter, and I just might." ॐTW

Kate Fetherston (aka "Mirabella") has been one of my most important writing companions. We both take immense pleasure in poem-crafting, and we delight in discovering extraordinary poets to share with one another. Because the mere thought of her reminds me of the joys of being a poet, penning a postcard to her is a perfect way for me to launch a writing session. What inspirational friend can *you* write to as a way of jump-starting the process?⸗MT

A

Way

to

Begin

POSTCARDS

Creating messages to fit in small spaces is a good way to sharpen our concentration. Postcards are short, informal letters that most people find fun and easy to write. For these exercises you will need a supply of postcards or blank 4" x 6" cards.

Postcards to People from Your Past

Write two of the following postcards.

* To the first person you kissed

* To a close childhood friend

* To a favorite teacher

* To a former enemy

Basic Exercise
(example on page 56)

Postcards to Nature

Write two of the following postcards.

* To a tree

* To a body of water

* To an animal

* To a mountain

Basic Exercise
(example on page 57)

Situational Postcards

Basic Exercise

(example on page 58)

Write two of the following postcards.

* Imagine you only have a short time to live. You are permitted to write one last postcard.

* Imagine that the only way out of a life-threatening situation is to write a postcard revealing a secret about yourself.

* Imagine you've been granted one wish, but must elucidate it on a postcard.

* Imagine that whatever you write on the postcard will be enacted as law.

For Partners: Using postcards to do Partner Writing is a good way to get your shared energies going. Choose someone you both know, or one of the postcard ideas from the above lists, and each write two lines on a postcard. Now exchange the cards. Read the lines to yourselves, and write the next two lines. Continue exchanging until it's time to sign your names, or some hybrid of your two names.

For Groups: This is an excellent exercise to do as individuals, sharing your results with the group. Or write group postcards (see "Circle Writing," page 28) as a quick way to produce a large number of entertaining pieces.

THE IMAGINARY VACATION

We all occasionally (or frequently) dream of taking a break from the routines of our lives by going on a vacation to a different place. This exercise uses the energy of wanderlust to get our words flowing.

Basic Exercise

(example on page 58)

1. Find a postcard of a place—a card someone sent you, or one from a local shop.

2. Study the card and imagine you are on vacation in that place.

3. Address the back of the postcard to a friend. Take a moment to visualize this friend.

4. Write a note telling your friend what you've been doing in that place, and what you're about to do.

VARIATION 1. Repeat the exercise (not necessarily from the same imaginary place), writing this card to a relative (mother, father, sibling).

VARIATION 2. Repeat the exercise (not necessarily from the same place), writing this card to yourself.

VARIATION 3. Repeat the exercise, writing a longer letter.

For Partners: Bring each other favorite or interesting postcards. Exchange them, and then do the exercise. Another variation: write your postcards to each other.

For Groups: Everyone bring one or two postcards. Shuffle the postcards and have each person randomly draw one to use for the exercise. For another variation, each of you can write a postcard to the entire group.

I like to keep a supply of actual postcards on my writing desk. I find the ritual of writing, addressing, and sending postcards an inspiring way to start my writing day. Knowing my words will be of interest to people I care about (and knowing how much we all like getting mail) is often all the motivation I need to get my writing day started.—TW

Ritual Postcards

FAMOUS PERSON EXERCISE

To do the Famous Person exercise you will need three sizes of blank cards: a business card, a postcard (4" x 6") and a standard page (8½" x 11").

Basic Exercise

(examples on pages 60–61)

1. Close your eyes and relax. Without forcing the process, allow the names of people you admire (not personal friends) to float into your consciousness. These people may be living or dead. They may be relatively obscure or known to millions. They may be authors or movie stars or religious leaders or politicians or musicians or artists. The essential thing is that you admire them.

2. When you've thought of several names, quickly write down three of them. Read these names aloud. Close your eyes again. Wait for one of these three names to stand out from the others. This is the person you will focus on for this exercise.

3. Imagine you're walking down a street and you see your famous person enter a house. As you linger on the sidewalk, the assistant of the person you admire comes out of the house and gives you a blank business card, saying, "Please write on this card who you are and why the person you admire might want to meet with you." You only have a minute or so to write your message.

4. The assistant disappears into the house with your card. A moment later, he emerges with good news. The person you admire is intrigued by what you wrote on the blank business card. He or she would like a bit more information. The assistant hands you a blank postcard and asks you to explain why the person you admire is important to you. Again, you only have a few minutes to fill the card.

5. Good news again. The famous person is on the verge of inviting you in for conversation and a cup of tea. But they want to know a little more about you. On a blank sheet of standard-size paper, write about yourself, keeping this famous person in mind.

Dear

Ray

I wrote my first letter to a famous person (Ray Charles) when I was ten. Ever since, I've written letters to artists I admire. Once in a great while I get a response from one of them, and a few have corresponded with me. But even when I get no response, expressing my feelings about their creations inspires and illuminates my creative process. ᠵ᠇TW

VARIATION 1. Choose a famous living person you admire. After you've done the three-card exercise, compose a letter and send it to him or her. (See "Sending Letters to Famous People" below.)

VARIATION 2. Choose a person you admire who is *not* famous (an ancestor, a friend, a teacher). Repeat the exercise using him or her as your focus.

Sending Letters to Famous People

So you've written a letter to that famous person you admire. Where do you send it?

- If the person is an author and they've written a *recently* published book, story, or article, send your letter to them care of (c/o) the publisher or publication.

- If the person is an author of a less recent book, do a book search on your library computer to see if they have a more recently published book. If they do, find the more recent book and send your letter to them c/o that publisher.

- If the person is a recording artist, send your letter to them c/o the record company. Check their album covers carefully for a fan-mail address.

- If the person is affiliated with a university, write them c/o the university at the department most likely to know them.

- If you've just heard the person on a live radio program, you can sometimes send your letter c/o the station and they will forward it. This is a long shot, so always have a backup copy of your letter so you can try another approach.

- If the person is a visual artist, write to them c/o the place where you saw their work, such as a gallery, publication, or museum.

- Another way to reach well-known people is through guilds or associations. For instance, many actors belong to the Screen Actors Guild, and some writers are members of the Authors Guild or the Writers Guild.

- Some people may not be as hard to reach as you think. If you know the city in which they live, you may find them listed in a telephone directory.

- You may be able to find a website for the person on the Internet. ⌁TW

Note: Whether or not your letter reaches that well-known person, the act of writing down your feelings and sending them out into the world is a valuable form of creative self-expression.

Examples

of

Letter

Forms

Exercises

Letters—*A Person I Know, Basic Exercise, page 46 (TW)*

Dear D.R.

I had a visit today from my charming friend James Norwood Pratt. We dined on Mexican food, spoke of the idiocy of American politics and the divine nature of existence, and then he departed for his home in North Beach. Moments later, a lovely card arrived in the mail—from you! The confluence of these events made me think how wonderful, and possibly overwhelming, it would be to bring the two of you together in the same room, Norwood being nearly as singular a character as you are, not to mention being a fine human being, as you are, too. And there is something about him that reminds me of you.

What something? Well, Norwood is passionate about ideas, has a vast knowledge of European history, and he makes no separation between his daily life and his art, his greatest creation being himself. He is a big handsome man in his mid-fifties with a deep, sonorous voice and a mischievous twinkle in his eye. He loves lyric poetry, overtly beautiful modern art, and exquisite details.

He is also an authority on tea and has been my teacher in the ways of tea for four years now, though I fear I am not a great student, having found myself stuck on one particular green tea to the exclusion of all others. The tea? Pi-lo Chün. An earthy green tea from China, the variety I adore being a Taiwan pretender. The *great* pretender.

Norwood and I like to talk about Buddhism and history and amazing things and people as we wander North Beach in quest of art and inexpensive Chinese food. He is far from wealthy, yet when we stood before a recent Wayne Thiebaud (have you seen his Delta paintings? Astonishing!) priced at five hundred and eighty-five thousand dollars, Norwood said with great sincerity, "A bargain at twice that."

He has also taken name-dropping to a new plane of poetic artistry, and every once in a while I know who he's talking about.

One day we must all assemble for tea.

Blessings and Love, Todd

Dear James,

I just wrote to my friend D.R. and gave him a description of you. It occurred to me that a meeting between the two of you would rank right up there with Groucho Marx meeting T. S. Eliot. (They were big fans of each other.)

D.R. is a petit point artist of some renown. His gorgeous rendering of a speeding train illustrates the cover of my novel, *Night Train*. When I first met D.R. his brown hair was splashed with a streak of blond. Now his hair is merely brown, but he is as colorful as ever. He's a wonderful poet, and he loves to improvise verbally, which is why I thought it might be fun to bring you two together, at your place, for tea and talk. At the very least, it will be great theater for me.

D.R. is absolutely dedicated to making his art and writing his poems. At a time in my life when I had almost no role model for my own brand of dedication, he was an important person for me to know. We performed together several times. I accompanied him on piano as he read his poems, and I wrote bursts of prose to accompany slide projections of his petit point creations. Big fun.

Anyway, D.R. is somehow kin to you, and I thought it would be good for you to meet him. You are both sensitive men, lovers of symmetry and surprise, fathers and poets. You both love good food and sharp insight. And neither of you goes by his given first name.

Soon, Todd

Letters—*Letter to Mother, Basic Exercise, page 47 (MT)*

Dear Edith:

After 23 years I have trouble remembering the sound of your voice or your easy laugh. When I think of you I usually feel sad, but I feel grateful, too. I wish I'd known you better, adult-to-adult, that the turbulence of our family life hadn't kept us so often confused and disconnected from ourselves and each other, not grounded in the moment.

Looking back, it seems amazing that you were able to impart to your children so much that is good. We've all turned out to be loyal and affectionate and funny. I think those things came largely from you. I think both your boys were deeply harmed by their military experiences, but still they are fundamentally kind and concerned with what's right. They are also smart and hard-working, yet capable of great playfulness.

They are mostly happy, I think, though their love lives haven't been easy. I'm the lucky one who found and married a true soulmate, a man who understands and respects and loves me totally. We're at 21 years, and counting!

I wish you were still around. We'd have a great time cooking together, singing and dancing, playing gin rummy and doing crosswords together like always, but also talking in a way we never did about what's in our hearts and giving each other a wise and mature kind of support.

All is well, and I love you, always.

Mindy

Postcard Exercises—*Postcards to People from Your Past, page 49*

To the first person you kissed

July 11, 1998

Dear Diana,

It has been forty-two years since you and I walked through the abandoned vineyard and climbed the old oak to a perch overlooking the overgrown grounds of the Erman estate. We were seven. We kissed and kissed until I grew dizzy. It didn't seem like child's play, but rather a glimpse into our future as sexually awakened beings. A pure exchange. Or so it seemed to me. Do you remember? I hope this finds you happy.

Love, Todd

TO:

DIANA

FIRST KISS

Place
Stamp
Here

To a favorite teacher

July 11, 1998

Dear Mrs. Davenport,

Todd here. I never knew your first name, though I loved you and wanted to marry. Third grade. You were tall and slender, black-haired, with a slow Oklahoma drawl. One day you told us you were one-sixteenth Cherokee, and I loved you all the more for that. You sang a cappella from a book of folk songs. You sat while you sang, and those of us who wanted to sing gathered around you and sang along. You made music and words come alive for me.

Blessings and Love, Todd

TO:

MRS. DAVENPORT

FAVORITE TEACHER

Place Stamp Here

Postcard Exercises—*Postcards to Nature, page 49*

To an animal

7-11-98

Dear Badger,

I still think of you often, or more precisely of your muzzle, that piece of yourself you sloughed off and left floating in clear water for me to find. I am still working on unmuzzling myself, without putting on any proud badges. You were and are an important guide. Come again, anytime.

Thanks, Mindy

TO:

DREAM BADGER

GREAT OCEAN OF

DREAMS

Place Stamp Here

Examples

of

Letter

Forms

Exercises

Postcard Exercises—*Situational Postcards, page 50*

A short time to live

7-11-98

Dear Bill and Randy,
I know you'll be sad when you find out I'm no longer alive in this world, but please don't dwell on it. I can't express how rich the experience of being your sister has been—not always easy or even comprehensible, but rich and real and extremely valuable. I know we were destined to be together in this life, which means we're likely to meet again. Meanwhile, remember who you really are, and rejoice.
Love Always, Mindy

Place
Stamp
Here

TO:
BILL AND RANDY
MY BROTHERS

The Imaginary Vacation—*Basic Exercise, page 50 (TW)*

Postcard of San Francisco

July 11, 1998

Dear Rico,
I've taken a few days to just hang out in San Francisco, North Beach to be precise. Thinking of you and the good old days here. Been to Café Trieste—fabulous cappuccinos—lunch at the Art Institute with all the pink- and purple-haired artistes, a poetry overdose at City Lights Books, spaghetti tonight at Little Joe's, and then I'll wander up to Coit Tower and write a poem or two with you in mind.
Yours Eternally, Murray

Place
Stamp
Here

TO:
RICO REES
A FRIEND

The Imaginary Vacation—*Basic Exercise, Variation 1,*
page 50

Postcard of Oregon beach

July 11, 1998
 	
Dear Dad,
   I'm sitting on a remote beach on the
Oregon Coast, a strong steady wind
blowing in off the sea. I've been camp-
ing here for a week now, sleeping so
soundly on the sand, I feel more rested
than I have in years. I'm drawing,
watching birds, writing short poems
about the grasses and waves and water.
I'm gonna walk into town to mail this
and get a crab burrito.
      Love, Todd
	Place
	Stamp
	Here
	
	To:
	CHARLES WALTON
	MY FATHER

The Imaginary Vacation—*Basic Exercise, Variation 2,*
page 51 (MT)

Postcard of Crete

July 11, 1998 *Well, Mindy, I wanted you to find this* *lovely reminder waiting for you in the* *mail. Crete has been everything we* *dreamed—the Aegean so warm and* *jewel-like, the food incredible (oh god,* *the sheep cheese!), the villagers as neu-* *tral toward our presence among them* *as I hoped. The writing has gone mar-* *velously, and Tad and I are younger* *than when we arrived. Remember to* *remember how it felt so you will return* *soon.* *Love, Your happiest self*	Place Stamp Here To: MYSELF

Famous Person Exercise—*Basic Exercise, page 51 (TW)*

Three famous people:
> *Bette Davis, Arthur Miller, Roland Hanna*

Choice of famous person:
> *Roland Hanna*

BUSINESS CARD:

Hello Roland Hanna: My name is Todd and I've admired your piano playing, your compositions, and your spirit for many years. I've heard you live a few times and count those nights among my best. I play piano, too.

POSTCARD:

Your freedom of expression, or maybe I should say your lack of inhibition when you improvise, and the surprising, always original results have been deeply inspiring for me. Not just for my own piano playing, but for my writing, my drawing, my cooking. It is so rare to encounter an artist of such refinement venturing into new territory *within* a form as you do. I'm not expressing this very well. Your music says so much to me, not in words, but in tone, in changes, in silences. You help me.

STANDARD-SIZE PAPER:

When I listen to your piano playing, particularly your solo work, I feel recognized. Or I recognize myself in there somehow. So much of the time the movies, books, music, and art that get all the attention seem to be about a world I have almost no feeling for, no connection with. When I write or play music, I'm listening for love and tenderness. I strive to tell stories with words and music that say what I feel your music says: "Be your true self. Open to the world. Don't be afraid to try things that might not sound like everything already has sounded."

And at the same time your music is imbued with your hundreds of thousands of hours of practice, as well as with the richness of your life dedicated to what you do. When I listen to you, I know that the sweetest moments come when we are gone to the gush of love, however it may manifest through us.

Famous Person Exercise—*Basic Exercise, page 51 (MT)*

Three famous people:

Deena Metzger, Georgia O'Keeffe, Daniel Berrigan

Choice of famous person:

Georgia O'Keeffe

BUSINESS CARD:

Ms. O'Keeffe: My name is Faith Greenbowl. I have learned to be with others in complete sympathetic silence. I would like to spend an afternoon walking with you in the red hills. I'll bring a fine oolong tea to inspire our talk.

POSTCARD:

Ms. O'Keeffe: Of course you know you have delighted and inspired countless people, with your paintings and with the example of your extraordinary life. I felt on first encountering your work that you had seen deeply into yourself and the world, as I—a gawky teenager—longed to do. The Great Mystery guides us in ways we can't fully comprehend to those beings who can show us a meaningful way to live. My eyes were opened by and to you long ago, and your flower visions, particularly, continue to nourish and enlighten me. I know we are destined to meet. Your sister in spirit, Faith Greenbowl

STANDARD-SIZE PAPER:

Ms. O'Keeffe: I, too, love the red earth and vast skies of the desert, where my mind and heart can expand beyond the arbitrary boundaries I buy into in the city. I, too, am an artist, in that I notice the world and take it into myself. I'm not afraid of getting lost or of opening completely to reveal everything. Flowers astonish and intoxicate me. They are my most important teachers. Clouds also mean a great deal to me; their constant shifting reminds me powerfully that all is impermanent and therefore precious, but not to be clung to. Simply noticing is enough. I write poems about these things. I sit or walk quietly. I love to sing. I have lost the habit of judging life as good or ill, pleasant or painful. I am told my presence is peace-engendering. Of course, on every level but the physical we are already friends, even sisters, maybe twins. Thank you for the beauty you offer to the world. Blessings, Faith Greenbowl

Chapter Four

$\mathcal{S}$TYLE

*Your style is an emanation
from your own being.*
—KATHERINE ANNE PORTER

e.e. cummings wrote, "As for expressing nobody-but-your-self in words, that means working just a little harder than anybody who isn't a poet can possibly imagine."

Whether you are a poet or a prose writer, or both, developing your unique voice, your nobody-but-yourself style, is one of the great rewards of your commitment to the writer's path.

The exercises in this chapter are intended to help you stretch the boundaries of your current writing style. We've included a number of exercises designed specifically to help poets make the transition to writing prose and exercises to help prose writers feel more at home writing poetry.

COPYING OUT POEMS AND PROSE

Something inexplicable and profound happens when we copy, by hand, a favorite poem or prose passage. Not only does our understanding of the words deepen, but we experience what it *feels* like to have a beloved creation flowing from our pens.

In this age of photocopiers and scanners, copying out a

poem or prose passage by hand may seem old-fashioned and needlessly time-consuming, but the purpose of hand copying is to follow in the footsteps of a master and thereby gain a deeper appreciation for the art of writing.

Basic Exercise	

1. Spend some time browsing through volumes of poetry or your favorite books of prose until you find a poem or passage you particularly admire.

2. In good light, with a favorite pen, copy out the passage. Take your time. Give each word your full attention. You may wish to pause after each line to assess your handiwork.

3. When you have finished copying out the words, read them aloud more than once, savoring the music of the language.

Here are a short poem and a prose fragment, either of which you may copy by hand to see what the process feels like.

SHORT POEM

Today, like every other day,
we wake up empty and frightened.
Don't open the door to the study
and begin reading. Take down
a musical instrument. Let
the beauty we love be what we do.
There are hundreds of ways
to kneel and kiss the ground.

— RUMI (TRANS. COLEMAN BARKS)

The rhythm of your phrasing is best revealed by reading your writing out loud.

PROSE PASSAGE

When the long winter nights come on and the wolves follow their meat into the lower valleys, he may be seen running at the head of the pack through the pale moonlight or glimmering borealis, leaping gigantic above his fellows, his great throat a-bellow as he sings a song of the younger world, which is the song of the pack.

—JACK LONDON, *The Call of the Wild*

WORD CHOICES

Mark Twain wrote, "As to the Adjective: when in doubt, strike it out." Whether or not one takes this literally, his underlying message is, "Why use a word if it doesn't contribute to the clarity or beauty or strength of a sentence?"

Another important aspect of word choice has to do with consistency. If your narrator—you or a persona you've assumed—uses only simple words for the first several pages of a story, it will seem out of character for her to suddenly use the word *esurient* instead of *hungry*. Consistency of language allows the reader to accept a narrator as real, which is essential to the enjoyment of written or spoken art.

Note: Chapter Five of this book, "Character," contains a number of exercises to help you invent and develop characters, each of whom will have a unique voice. The following exercises can be done in the voice of any character you invent.

Toying With Words

1. Quickly and playfully write a simple sentence.

2. Replace all the nouns with new nouns.

3. Place an adjective in front of each noun.

4. Change all the words except for the nouns and adjectives.

5. Change all the adjectives.

6. Place an adverb in front of each verb.

7. Place an adjective in front of each adjective.

8. Make all the nouns plural. (If any are already plural, make them singular.)

9. Change all the nouns, and half the adjectives.

10. Change any four of the words.

11. Use your final sentence as the first sentence of a paragraph. Try to write in a style that feels consistent with the style of this sentence.

> *Basic Exercise*
> (example on page 81)

VARIATION 1. Complete the basic exercise, then strike out all the adjectives that don't sound quite right to you. Use this sentence as the style-setting first sentence of a paragraph.

VARIATION 2. Look over each step of your exercise and choose the sentence you like best. Make this the style-setting first sentence of a paragraph.

Note: A thesaurus or dictionary may come in handy for these exercises.

Adjective or Noun?

In the quotation at the beginning of this chapter, Mark Twain is suggesting that an adjective is often undesirable when a more precise *noun* would suffice. For instance, a more precise way of saying *deep, steep-sided valley* is the word *chasm*. This exercise is a way to practice verbal precision.

ℬasic Exercise
(example on page 81)

1. Do five minutes of free-writing (see page xiv) or use a poem or prose passage you've already written.

2. Choose a paragraph, or ten lines of a poem, containing adjectives. Read the passage aloud.

3. Delete all the adjectives and read the passage aloud again.

4. Identify which nouns are no longer precise enough in their meaning. Think of other nouns that convey by themselves what your original noun could convey only with the help of an adjective.

5. Rewrite your piece to accommodate any replacement nouns you decide to use. Where you can't think of more precise nouns, keep your originals. Read the new paragraph or poem aloud.

6. Rewrite your paragraph or poem, using adjectives wherever they sound good to you. Read aloud.

VARIATION 1. Repeat steps 1 and 2. For step 3, replace all nouns with other nouns that work well with your existing adjectives. For step 4, delete all your adjectives and read your poem or prose passage aloud. Any nouns you want to change? Any adjectives you want to put back?

Time and again with my own writing, and in working with other writers, I have been amazed and heartened by what happens when we rewrite a prose piece or a poem from a different perspective—in another person or tense, or another person *and* tense.

For instance, here is a passage in third person, past tense.

He was a small man, quick-witted and good-natured. He made his living cleaning houses four days a week. The rest of his time he spent writing poetry and corresponding with well-known poets, most of whom declined to answer his passionate missives.

Here is the passage, reworked in first person, present tense.

I don't think of myself as small when I'm alone, or when I'm with Flo. She's an inch shorter than I am. It's only when I'm out in the world that I realize most men are taller than I. Not that I mind, really. All the tall men I know have back problems, a fate I've been spared.

I clean houses four days a week, and it gives me enough money to pay the rent and keep our bellies full. I work on my poems on Fridays and Saturdays. Sundays are reserved for time with Flo. We usually go on a long walk in the morning and catch a movie matinee. Then we'll eat Chinese and spend the evening reading to each other, or making love.

I got a letter yesterday from Quinton Duval, the poet. He said a very nice thing about one of my poems. He said it made him remember an incident from his childhood he hadn't thought about in over twenty years. I feel honored he wrote me. It makes me feel less alone as a poet.

There may be times when the tone created by a first-person narrator feels too personal or intimate for a particular subject or story, and a shift to third person can make the writing flow more easily. I have crafted a number of stories by writing the first draft in first person, present tense, then rewriting in third person, present tense, then reworking again in third person, past tense. Each shift gives me a fresh perspective, allowing new ideas and details to emerge.∽TW

Person and Tense Shifting

LINE LENGTHS IN POEMS

Note: Certain traditional poetry forms dictate precisely where lines end. If you're writing in iambic pentameter, for example, the decision is made before you begin. For poets writing free verse, however, the possibilities are limitless. (Consult your dictionary, encyclopedia, or a book about classical poetic forms for precise definitions of *iambic* and *pentameter.*)

Some poets say the rhythm of the poem determines where one line ends and the next begins. Others say their line breaks are arbitrary—that they write a poem without worrying about line length, then decide on a length that looks good on the page. They copy their poem into that format, letting the breaks fall where they may.

Some poets break their lines where they want the reader to pause, or where they've completed a thought or a breath. They might end a line with a period, a comma, or a dash if they wish the pause to be a bit longer.

Most poets use a combination of these techniques to shape their poems.

Arbitrary Line Lengths

Basic Exercise
(example on page 83)

1. Write five to ten lines of poetry or poetic prose. For the purpose of this exercise, a line is defined as the width of whatever page you're using. You can use one of the Sketching exercises, page 30, to help you create a poem. Or you can free-write for five minutes, then choose a passage you particularly like.

2. Copy the chosen lines into a new format, with each line two inches wide.

3. Read your poem in this form and make any changes that occur to you.

4. Copy your poem into a new format, with each line four inches wide.

5. Read your poem in this form and make any changes that occur to you.

6. Copy your poem into a new format, with each line six inches wide.

7. Read your poem in this form and make any changes that occur to you.

8. Review the evolution of your poem. Which format do you prefer? Did you find that one line length inspired more revisions than another?

VARIATION 1. Complete Step 1 of the Basic Exercise. Reverse the order of the format shifts in the Basic Exercise, beginning with the longer lines and making them progressively shorter.

VARIATION 2. Try all the different line length formats before changing any words in your poem. Choose the length that appeals to you most and rewrite your poem in that format.

VARIATION 3. Create an arbitrary line length form with two *different* lengths. For example, make your first four lines three inches long, and then have two lines two inches in length, and so on.

Line Length by Rhythm

1. Write a single line of poetry. Read the line aloud to get a feel for its rhythm.

Basic Exercise

2. Write a second line for your poem, with a length and rhythm similar to that of your first line. Read your two lines aloud.

3. Write a third line for your poem, matching the rhythm and length you've established in the first two lines. Read your three lines aloud.

4. Revise these first three lines, if necessary, to make them sound rhythmically consistent.

5. Write three more lines that match the rhythm and length of your first three lines.

VARIATION 1. Complete step 1. Make your second line shorter than the first—but harmonious with it. Make your third line match the length and rhythm of your first line, make your fourth line match the length and rhythm of your second line, and so forth.

VARIATION 2. Before writing anything down, say a line out loud—anything that comes to mind. For example, "Honey, Bernice is on the phone" or "There was something in the dark at the top of the stairs." Use this spontaneously spoken line to establish the cadence and length of your first line. Now complete the subsequent steps of the basic exercise.

Variation 3. When you've made a poem you like, use it for one of the Arbitrary Line Length exercises.

The Poetics of Necessity

A friend gave me a chapbook of poetry by a little-known poet. I became an instant fan. His writing was humorous and wholly original. The lines of his poems were all short—never more than five words in length. I was curious about why he broke his lines as he did. Such short lines created a staccato effect—a rapid-fire series of images and ideas.

When I heard he was reading in a café near my house, I went to hear him. He was an enormous man, suffering from emphysema. His lines broke precisely where he needed to take a breath in order to continue reading.∽TW

Line Length by Breath

Basic Exercise

1. Write five to ten lines of poetry or poetic prose. For the purpose of this exercise, a line length is defined by the width of whatever page you're using. You may free-write for five minutes, then select a passage you particularly like.

2. Take a breath and read aloud, at a comfortable pace, as much of your poem as you can with a single breath. Note the word at which you felt the need to take another breath. Make this word the last word of your first line.

3. Break the rest of your poem into lines roughly the same length as this first line.

4. Read your entire poem aloud, reading each line with a single breath. If you find yourself growing short of breath in the process of reading the poem, shorten the length of your lines so you can comfortably read the entire poem at a pace of one breath per line.

5. Revise your poem so the rhythm of the lines is consistent.

VARIATION 1. Break your poem into a long-breath line, followed by a short-breath line, and so on. Revise the poem within this format.

VARIATION 2. Create a poem using one of the Arbitrary Line Length techniques. Practice reading it so that you use one breath for each line, no matter how short the lines.

SENTENCE LENGTHS

Sentence length is a primary aspect of style. Some writers use short sentences. Or sentence fragments. They just do. Other writers extend their sentences over many lines, breaking them with commas, colons, semi-colons, and dashes—as if to avoid the sense of finality a period imparts to a line of thought. Some writers begin their paragraphs with short sentences and end them with longer ones. Some writers don't think at all about the lengths of their sentences.

There are no rights or wrongs about sentence length, but it is helpful to understand the effect of sentence length on the tone and pace of your prose.

Arbitrary Sentence Lengths

1. Close your eyes and imagine you are someone who writes in short sentences. These need not be complete sentences.

2. Using short sentences, write about something that recently happened to you, or make up a story. Write a half-page or so. Read aloud.

3. Close your eyes again. Imagine you are a person who writes in longer sentences.

4. Using your short sentence passage as a rough draft, rewrite your story using longer sentences.

VARIATION 1. Reverse this process, and begin by imagining you are someone who writes in longer sentences, then rewrite using shorter sentences.

> *Basic Exercise*
> (examples on pages 85–86)

VARIATION 2. Take a preexisting prose piece, or something you've created while free-writing, and revise it using either shorter or longer sentence lengths.

For Partners: Each of you write a short-sentence draft, then exchange stories and each rewrite the other's story using longer sentences.

Splitting and Reversing Lines

When I rewrite a poem or prose passage, splitting my lines gives my eyes and brain a new form to work with, and this newness often helps break a verbal logjam. For instance, if I write

a gray heron sat on a dead branch above the muddy river

I might split the line in half, or into three parts.

a gray heron sat tucked into himself
on a dead branch high
above the muddy river

Splitting existing lines by leaving blank lines between them can also be a useful rewriting technique. For instance, if I write

He never believed her when she called him sweetie
because her voice was always so full of bitterness

then I can split the lines to see what might fall between them.

He never believed her when she called him sweetie.
How could he believe her
~~because~~ when *her voice was always ~~so~~ full of bitterness?*

Another way to play with lines is to reverse them.

because her voice was always full of bitterness.
He never believed her when she called him sweetie

~~because~~ *her voice* ~~was always~~ *full of bitterness*
~~H~~he ~~never~~ couldn't ~~believed~~ *her when she called him sweetie*

her voice full of bitterness,
he couldn't believe her when she called him sweetie

—TW

POETRY FROM PROSE

Somehow, somewhere along our paths, many of us develop an aversion to poetry—to reading it and to writing it. This aversion to poems is absent in most young children. With minimal guidance, all of the young people we've worked with write poetry with ease and delight. Given our young students' unmitigated affinity for poetic forms, we have tapped their wisdom by asking, "What is a poem?"

Of the many delightful answers we've received, our favorites are:

- "Words that make a picture."

- "A short story in a pattern."

- "The same as other writing only you break up the lines in a rhythm."

Words That Make a Picture

1. Do ten minutes of free-writing.

2. As you read through your writing, underline any particularly potent words, phrases, or passages that you want to work with. These powerful words may be thought of as fragments of poetry embedded in prose.

3. Transfer these words, in the order in which they were written, to a blank piece of paper.

4. Craft a poem from these words.

VARIATION 1. Choose an arbitrary line length to give yourself a format in which to fit your words. You can always change the line lengths later, if you wish.

VARIATION 2. Start each line of your poem with one of the words you've gleaned from your free-writing.

> *Basic Exercise*
> (example on page 87)

A Short Story in a Pattern

<table>
<tr>
<td>

Basic Exercise

(example on page 89)

</td>
<td>

1. Write a short prose passage—perhaps an interesting episode from your life, a bit of fiction, or a reflection on the state of the world.

2. Copy your sentences onto a fresh sheet of paper, with each sentence starting a new line on the page.

3. Craft these sentences into the lines of a poem, adding, subtracting, or changing words as you get into the rhythm of your poetry.

4. Give your poem a title.

5. Wait a day, read your poem aloud, then rewrite it if you wish.

</td>
</tr>
</table>

Breaking Prose Lines in a Rhythm

<table>
<tr>
<td>

Basic Exercise

(example on page 91)

</td>
<td>

1. Write a burst of prose.

2. Decide on an arbitrary line length and copy your prose to fit into that format.

3. Craft a poem from these lines.

4. Wait an hour, then read what you've crafted.

5. Title your poem and rewrite, if you wish.

</td>
</tr>
</table>

<table>
<tr>
<td>

Dear

Prose

Writer

</td>
<td>

The exercises here are experiments in the bare essentials of poetic form. But poetry is more than a particular structure applied to a piece of writing. At their finest, poems wake us up. They broaden our perspective to include the whole cosmos, even if the subject of the poem is something tiny, like an insect or a seed. You could spend a lifetime—many writers have—crafting poems that open the heart, expand the mind, nourish the soul. As a beginning, let yourself simply play.—MT

</td>
</tr>
</table>

PROSE FROM POETRY

Many fine poets express trepidation about turning their writing talents to prose, either fiction or nonfiction. This trepidation often springs from the understanding that poetry and prose are very different kinds of writing. Yet great prose is, in essence, poetic, *and* many of the most revered poems tell stories. Here is an exercise to help you make the transition from writing poetry to writing prose.

Basic Exercise (example on page 93)

1. Write a poem of three to nine lines, or use a favorite poem you've already written.

2. Copy your poem onto a page (or pages), leaving a third of the page blank after each line. You'll wind up with three lines to a page. If your poem is longer than nine lines, use only the first nine lines for this process. As you copy your lines, begin to think of them as prose.

3. Write a first paragraph that flows from your first line. Feel free to modify the first line to make it work grammatically or to fit the flow of the paragraph.

4. Using the second line of your poem as the beginning of your second paragraph, continue your story. Again, feel free to modify the line to make it work grammatically or to fit the flow of the developing story.

5. Continue this process until you've completed a prose paragraph beginning with each line of your poem.

6. Read your creation aloud. If you like what you've written so far, expand and refine it.

VARIATION 1. Some poets compose poems in couplets (groupings of two lines) or stanzas (distinct sections separated by blank lines). You may use couplets or entire stanzas as beginnings for the different parts of your story.

VARIATION 2. Make each of your lines the *end* of a paragraph.

Note: Though it may seem that narrative poems—those that tell stories—would be more appropriate for this poem-to-prose process, that isn't necessarily the case. Purely imagistic poetry can underpin a lovely story. In fact, the evocative line *flaming red scarf* may be more inspiring than *A man was stuck in Lodi.*

Writers are lovers of language, which makes most of us avid readers. Since learning to read we have gobbled up countless novels and essays, stories, plays and poems. In the process we have been unavoidably influenced by the writing of others. Our favorite authors, especially, have inspired and informed us. Yes, each one of us is a creative being unique in all of time, but our work can't help but carry some hint of our literary heroes.

This imprinting happens gradually and beneath our conscious awareness, so its effect on our writing is often subtle. Occasionally, though, we seem to be writing *as* a favorite author. Here's a story from my own writing practice.

One day my husband and I set out for a day of hiking on beautiful Mount Tamalpais. We had recently checked out an audio tape from the library: Emily Dickinson's nature poems recited over a background of natural sounds—birds whistling, a stream tinkling, waves crashing on rocks, a cricket chirping. Listening to this tape as we drove to the trailhead put us both in an open, reverent frame of mind. We listened to the tape twice through, so nourishing was this immersion in the words of a long-dead poet who felt a deep kinship with the natural world. I recalled how enraptured with Dickinson's poems I had been as a teenager and spoke to my husband about this early literary love. By the time we reached our destination, I felt thoroughly steeped in Emily.

It was an idyllic day in early spring. Purple lupine and golden poppies spread themselves out lavishly on the hillsides. As I stepped onto the trail, the vast blue Pacific far below, I was so overcome with the beauty of the moment that I found myself in tears. After two hours of wandering, my heart and mind were full to overflowing, and a poem wrote itself in my head, a poem very much in the spirit of Emily Dickinson. I had taken her in so deeply just prior to our walk that her voice seemed to speak in my poem. Here it is:

POPPIES
If all we had were poppies, still
our longing should be met
for flowers offer to the heart
ecstatic nourishment.
Yet we pass by. The trail's arm
is long and points away.
Tomorrow calls, "come follow," while
the moment murmurs, "stay."

Try this for yourself. Spend hours or days reading a writer you greatly admire, taking her deeply into yourself. Then sit down to write. Something of her skill and wisdom and beauty may flow from your pen.⁓MT

FOUND POEMS

Found poems are made from words or phrases *not* originally intended to be poetry, but perceived as poetry by the writer who finds them. For example, while reading a very old dictionary, we came upon a definition for the word *give* that sounded like a poem. The original passage looked like this:

> *give*
> The basal meaning of this verb, from which all others spring, seems to be the transference or passing of something, good or bad, material or non-material, without any implication of exchange...

We modified the lines thusly:

> *give*
> The basal meaning of this verb,
> from which all others spring,
> seems to be the transference
> of something, good or bad,
> material or non-material,
> without implication of exchange

Found poems may also result from interesting juxtapositions of words or lines you happen to notice in everyday life.

For instance, one morning, his stomach growling, Todd shuffled into the kitchen and found the various sections of the newspaper spread open like a hand of cards. The business section trumpeted *Markets Tumble*. The sports section proclaimed *Giants Stumble*. The international news section warned *Mt. Etna Rumbles*. And the entertainment section headlined a book review: *But What Does It All Mean?*

His found poem went like this.

As My Stomach Grumbles
Markets tumble,
Giants stumble,
Mt. Etna rumbles.
But what does it all mean?

Note: Though the following exercises make suggestions for how to go about finding and creating Found Poems, our experience has been that many of the best found poems appear when we're *not* looking for them. But even if deliberate searching doesn't turn up any found poems you love, you'll still be primed to recognize them when they do appear.

Entering an art museum, Mindy stood before the sign announcing the show she'd come to see. Big bold letters read VISIONS OF THE APOCALYPSE. To the right of the sign was a doorway marked EMERGENCY EXIT. Hence her found poem:

ART
Visions of the Apocalypse.
Emergency.
Exit.

Sometimes what we find are not so much poems as titles for poems. Here are some favorite found titles:

Rough Road Ahead (road sign)
What's Holding You Back? (billboard)
If Someone Can Claim You (income tax form)
Razor Point (words on a box of pens)

Headline Combinations

Basic Exercise

1. Get a newspaper.

2. Go through it and write down any headlines that sound good or funny or interesting to you.

3. Combine them in various ways to make a poem.

Juxtapositions and Combinations

Basic Exercise

1. When you're walking or biking or driving around, jot down slogans from billboards, directives from road signs, snatches of overheard conversations, titles of musical recordings, flyers, bumper stickers—anything that catches your eye or ear.

2. Combine some of your jottings to make a poem.

Word Choices—*Toying with Words, Basic Exercise, page 67 (TW)*

1. A man walked into a store.

2. A cat walked into a bedroom.

3. A black cat walked into a small bedroom.

4. The black cat snuck around the small bedroom.

5. The gray cat snuck around the humid bedroom.

6. The gray cat stealthily snuck around the humid bedroom.

7. The enormous gray cat stealthily snuck around the horribly humid bedroom.

8. The enormous gray cats stealthily snuck around the horribly humid bedrooms.

9. The devious gray trolls stealthily snuck around the hideously humid dungeon.

10. Seven deviously neurotic trolls stealthily crept around the hideously humid dungeon.

11. Seven deviously neurotic trolls stealthily crept around the hideously humid dungeon. Their grotesquely potent names were Althazar, Balthazar, Calthazar, Morgren, Salgaron, Malgaron, and Snorf. They were insidiously plotting the death of the dark and terrible tyrant of their crumbling castle, Lord Hysteria. Althazar, he of the toxic garlic breath, favored poisoning their most hated overlord with the noxious bile of a counter-phobic wart-covered nymph. The other vile trolls favored slow, gut-wrenching death by multiple, nefarious curses.

Word Choices—*Adjectives, Basic Exercise, page 68 (TW)*

1 and 2. Paragraph chosen from free-writing session.

My beleaguered desk has reached that chaotic state where meaningful work is now impossible. I sit before the raucous seascape of paper and torn envelopes raised up on hidden rubber stamps and dull-bladed scissors, empty pens and dog-eared dictionaries. I know if I am ever to finish anything ever again, I must focus my wandering mind on making order instead of making more new poems I cannot type because my filthy keyboard lies deep beneath the murky surface of so much left undone.

3 and 4. Delete all adjectives; identify imprecise nouns.

My desk has reached that *state* where *work* is now impossible. I sit before the seascape of *paper* and *envelopes* raised up on rubber stamps and *scissors, pens* and dictionaries. I know if I am to finish *anything* ever again, I must focus my *mind* on making order instead of making more poems I cannot type because the keyboard lies beneath the surface of so much left undone.

5.   Rewrite with more precise nouns.

My desk is in chaos, wordsmithing now impossible. I sit before the seascape of verbiage and envelopes raised up on the paraphernalia of my trade, knowing if I am ever to finish another poem, I must focus on making order instead of making more poems. I cannot type because the keyboard lies beneath the surface of so much left undone.

6.   Rewrite again, inserting adjectives where desired.

My desk has reached a state of total chaos from which I cannot hope to extract another poem. I sit before a frozen seascape of verbiage raised high on the hidden paraphernalia of my trade—pens, rubber stamps, scissors, envelopes, calendar and dictionaries—and I know if I am ever to send forth another finished poem, I must give myself to making order. Yes, before the sea of paper overflows the boundaries of my desk, I must file, and recycle, and raise my trusty tools to the surface of so much left undone.

Line Lengths in Poems—*Arbitrary Line Lengths, Basic Exercise, page 70 (MT)*

1. Write some lines of poetic prose.

    In August, the creek slows down to a
    sweet and sultry somersault over stones
    and berry brambles, not hurrying
    someplace else. Its music is gentle
    and persuasive. Listening, my heart
    settles down, rests content in
    the fullness of summer.

2. Two-inch-wide format (when hand-written).

    In August the creek
    slows down to a sweet
    and sultry somersault
    over stones and berry
    brambles, not hurrying
    someplace else. Its music
    is gentle and persuasive.
    Listening, my heart
    settles down, rests
    content in the fullness
    of summer.

3. Minor changes made.

    In August the creek
    slows down to a sweet
    and sultry somersault
    over stones and berry
    brambles, not hurrying
    someplace else. ~~Its music~~
    ~~is gentle and persuasive.~~
    Listening, my heart
    settles down, rests
    ~~content~~ in the fullness
    of summer.

4. Four-inch-wide format (when hand-written).

In August the creek slows down
to a sweet and sultry somersault
over stones and berry brambles,
not hurrying someplace else.
Listening, my heart settles down,
rests in the fullness of summer.

5. Minor changes made.

In August the creek slows down
to a ~~sweet and~~ sultry somersault
over stones and berry brambles,
not hurrying someplace else.
Listening, my heart settles down,
rests in the fullness of summer.

6. Six-inch-wide format (when hand-written).

In August the creek slows down to a sultry
somersault over stones and berry brambles,
not hurrying someplace else. Listening,
my heart settles down, rests in the fullness
of summer.

7. Minor changes made.

In August the creek becomes a sultry
somersault over stones and brambles,
not hurrying someplace else. Listening,
my heart settles down, rests content,
in the warm abundance of summer.

8. Review evolution.

My favorite version is the one that came out of step 4. The words of the poem seemed to want to fall into a certain spoken rhythm, and the four-inch width got closest to sounding musical to me (like a creek might sound in late summer).

Sentence Lengths—*Basic Exercise, page 73 (MT)*

1 and 2. Short sentence draft.

MELODY

Went out last night. To a recital. Met Melody. Melody sings mezzo soprano. She's Chinese. She's tiny. She has a lisp. A cute lisp. She studies piano. With a voice like that, piano? A guest approached her. He spoke in Chinese, her very dialect. She was delighted. Later, she played a guitar. She's so small. So much talent!

3 and 4. Longer sentence draft.

MELODY

Peter and Tony just bought a house, a large one high on a hill, looking out across the bay toward the Golden Gate Bridge. Last night, I attended a recital there of Tony's voice students. There were perhaps ten performers, but I was most intrigued by Melody.

She is a diminutive Chinese woman who sings extraordinary mezzo soprano despite a pronounced yet utterly charming lisp. To her great delight, one of the guests—an impeccably dressed but somewhat peculiar Chinese man—spoke her same, rare Chinese dialect.

She speaks English quite well and is friendly with the other students, but it seemed to relax her to converse for a few moments in her native tongue. At my coaxing, she led the group in an odd but beautiful English round she had mentioned she knew. Later, she picked up a guitar, and with a couple of pointers from Tad, was able to play an old Fleetwood Mac tune within minutes.

I admit I was a bit awestruck by her. How can so much talent and enthusiasm and vigor and sheer joy inhabit such a tiny person? Obviously her spirit is vast. I asked for her story, but she would only say that she lives in San Francisco's Chinatown, and that her parents are very traditional.

Sentence Lengths—*Basic Exercise, page 73 (TW)*

1 and 2. Short sentence draft.

NO MUFFINS

I go to the bakery every morning. I always get coffee and a muffin. Sometimes I get bran, sometime blueberry. Today they were out of both kinds. It really threw me off. I didn't know what to get. I felt nervous. I even felt a little paranoid. I felt like I was doing something wrong. Even illegal. I got my coffee. I thought that would calm me down. But I felt naked with just coffee. I needed something else. I looked at the display case. Everything blurred together. I couldn't believe how confused I felt. Then Donna said she'd found one last bran muffin. I felt so relieved I almost cried. I sat on the bench in front of the bakery. Like I always do. Benny to my right, Myrtle to my left. Everything was the same a usual. But I felt elated. I finished my muffin and coffee. I went back inside. Things weren't blurry anymore. I really liked the look of the oatmeal cookies. If they run out of my muffins again, I have a fall-back plan now.

3 and 4. Longer sentence draft.

NO MUFFINS

I've been going to my neighborhood bakery, Toots Sweet, every morning for the past seventeen years. I always get the same thing—a large coffee, black, and a muffin, either bran or blueberry. But today they were out of both kinds, and it really threw me off. I stared at the display case, desperate to think of something else to order, but everything blurred together. I couldn't tell the croissants from the bearclaws, the turnovers from the sticky buns. I felt out of control, like I'd been caught doing something horribly illegal. I blushed and stammered, and without thinking, I turned away from the counter and got myself a big cup of coffee. I guess I figured keeping to some part of my routine would calm me down, but it didn't. I felt positively naked with just coffee and nothing to eat.

And then Donna, who I've secretly lusted after for the last eleven years, said she's found one last bran muffin at the back of the last rack at the very back of the bakery. I felt so relieved, I almost cried. I could have kissed her, except the counter was between us and her husband is a former prizefighter. Then I stumbled outside to sit on the old bench with Benny and Myrtle, the pigeons chortling around us on the sidewalk. A day like any other, sure, but I felt elated, like I'd had a death sentence lifted. Everything Benny said was hilarious, and everything Myrtle said seemed laden with mystical import. I was vividly aware of the astonishing details of life, and I noticed for the first time—really noticed—what Benny was eating with his coffee. A big, fat oatmeal cookie. And then I knew, if they ever ran out of my muffins again, what I'd get instead.

Poetry from Prose—*Words That Make a Picture, Basic Exercise, page 75 (MT)*

1 and 2. Free-writing, selected words underlined.

<u>Carl</u> tells me <u>stories</u> that wake me up somehow. He's got three decades on me, but his attitude is <u>vibrant</u> and his mind quick. I encountered him this morning, <u>sunning himself</u> on a bench in front of the cafe, and sat for a moment while he told me about his millionaire nephew's wedding. "Seventy-thousand bucks for <u>one celebration!</u> What a scandal!" He grew up in New York, <u>in the days</u> of the Art Students' League and the Wobblies. He says it was romantic, <u>hanging out with communists</u> and other intellectuals, <u>speaking out</u> from corner soapboxes. He says his wife refused him the first time he proposed, but <u>he convinced her</u> to take a chance. Forty years later, he lived for weeks <u>by her bedside</u> as she died of breast cancer. "<u>Money</u> doesn't make a happy marriage," he tells me. "<u>People have to learn</u> not to be so selfish!" I could <u>kiss</u> him for his <u>wisdom</u> and his inspiration, but he'd probably think I was making a pass.

3. List selected words on blank paper.

> Carl
> stories
> vibrant
> sunning himself
> in the days
> one celebration
> hanging out with communists
> speaking out
> he convinced her
> by her bedside
> money
> people have to learn
> kiss
> wisdom

4. Poem crafted from selected words.

> *I listen, enthralled, to Carl's vibrant stories,*
> *as he suns himself on a cafe bench:*
> *"I hung out with communists,*
> *in the old days,*
> *lectured from soapboxes,*
> *married late."*
>
> *Forty years later (a decade ago),*
> *by his dying wife's bedside*
> *he wept and spoke vows*
> *it was too late to keep.*
>
> *"Wisdom doesn't come*
> *from the happy times,"*
> *he assures me this bright September morning*
> *and gives me a kiss right on the lips.*
> *"But happiness comes to the wise."*

Poetry from Prose—*A Short Story in a Pattern, Basic Exercise, page 76 (TW)*

1. Prose passage.

I waited all morning for the refrigerator repair person to come. He never showed up. I called the dispatcher and she said the repair person was scheduled to come tonight. I was furious because I'd canceled an important appointment to be here when the repair person arrived. I tried to look on the bright side of things. Maybe I wasn't supposed to go out into the world today. Maybe I would have been killed if I'd gone out. Or maybe the one thing the repair person needed to know in order to fix my refrigerator, he learned while on another job while I was waiting for him.

2. Make each sentence a separate line.

I waited all morning for the refrigerator repair person to come.
He never showed up.
I called the dispatcher and she said the repair person was scheduled to come tonight.
I was furious because I'd canceled an important appointment to be here when the repair person arrived.
I tried to look on the bright side of things.
Maybe I wasn't supposed to go out into the world today.
Maybe I would have been killed if I'd gone out.
Or maybe the one thing the repair person needed to know in order to fix my refrigerator, he learned while on another job while I was waiting for him.

3. Craft a poem.

> *Waiting all morning for the repair man,*
> *I listened to records I hadn't played in years.*
> *The repair man never showed up.*
>
> *Fearing my food would spoil in my dying*
> *refrigerator, I called the dispatcher. She said,*
> *"There must be some mistake. Harry isn't*
> *scheduled to come to your house until tonight."*

*I slammed down the phone. I'd canceled my
lunch date with Yvonne to be home for Harry.
I felt duped by fate. My life seemed full of mistakes.*

*I listened to an old Miles Davis album and tried
to look on the bright side of things. Maybe I wasn't
supposed to go out into the world today. Maybe I would
have been killed if I'd gone out.*

*Or maybe while Harry was on that other job, he
learned what he needed to know to fix my refrigerator.
Maybe my staying home was the key.*

4 and 5: Title and rewrite.

HARRY

*Waiting all morning for the repair man,
I listened to records I hadn't played in years.
The repair man never showed up.*

*Fearing my food would spoil in my sputtering
refrigerator, I called the dispatcher. She said,
"There must be some mistake. Harry isn't
scheduled to come to you until tonight."*

*I hung up, furious. I'd canceled my
lunch date with Yvonne to be home for Harry.
My life seemed to be an endless cycle of mistakes.*

*I listened to an old Miles Davis album. I tried
to look on the bright side of things. Maybe I wasn't
supposed to go out today.
Maybe I would have
been killed if I'd gone driving.*

*Or perhaps while I was waiting for Harry he was
learning what he needed to know to fix my fridge.
Maybe staying home was the key.*

Poetry from Prose—*Breaking Prose Lines in a Rhythm,*
Basic Exercise, page 76 (TW)

1. Burst of prose.

There are days when I feel a restlessness I have no explanation
for. Does my body want to go for a walk? Is there someone I
need to talk to? Is there something I need to change about
myself? Or is restlessness merely part of what makes us
human? So I go for a walk, and if the restlessness lingers, I call
the first person who comes to mind. If I reach them, and we
talk, and I still feel unsettled, I make a list of things I've been
putting off. If one thing on my list shouts louder than the others, I endeavor to do it. And as a last resort, I read a few poems,
and then take another walk, releasing my need to know anything for certain.

2. Arbitrary line length

   There are days when I feel a restlessness I have no
   explanation for. Does my body want to go for a walk?
   Is there someone I need to talk to? Is there something
   I need to change about myself? Or is restlessness merely
   part of what makes us human? So I go for a walk, and
   if the restlessness lingers, I call the first person who
   comesto mind. If I reach them, and we talk, and I
   still feel unsettled, I make a list of things I've been
   putting off. If one thing on my list shouts louder than
   the others, I endeavor to do it. And as a last resort, I
   read a few poems, and then take another walk,
   releasing my need to know anything for certain.

3. Craft a poem from these lines.

   Days when I feel a restlessness I have no
   explanation for I ask these questions. Does
   my body wish to go for a walk? Is there
   someone I crave to speak to? Is there
   something in myself I want to change? Or is
   restlessness merely what makes us human?

I take that walk, and if the restlessness lingers, I call the first person who comes to mind. And if after speaking to them, I still feel unsettled, I make a list of things I think I should do, and I endeavor to do the one thing that shouts louder than the others.

As a last resort, I will read a poem, then take another walk, letting go of my need to know.

4 and 5: Title poem and rewrite.

MY NATURE

Days when I feel restless, I ask myself these questions. Does my body wish to walk? Is there someone I crave to contact? Is there something in me I want to change? Or is this unease what makes me human?

I walk into the hills. Should my restlessness linger, I try to reach the person who appears most clearly in my mind. And if speaking to them does not settle me, I make a list of all the things I think I should do, and hope to heed the loudest call.

As a last resort, I will read a poem, then take another walk, untethering my need to know.

Prose from Poetry—*Basic Exercise, page 77 (TW)*

1. The poem

HOW IT PASSES

My father's brother says that love is a healing ray,
a physical wave as yet undetected by scientists,
that flows from human to human,
endlessly and freely,
unless we are afraid.

2 through 5. The lines of the poem as beginnings to paragraphs
   of a prose piece:

My father's brother says that love is a healing ray. I
was seventeen when he first told me this. At the time, I
thought he was being his usual inscrutable self. As far as I was
concerned, love was a form of desperation, a force compelling
me to try to win the attention, the devotion, and the kisses of
a lovely girl—any lovely girl would do. And yet something in
the way my uncle spoke about love made me think he knew
something I might benefit from knowing.

"A physical wave as yet undetected by scientists," he
added, smiling enigmatically through the steam rising from his
mug of coffee. "There are countless so-called mystical ideas
that will one day be visible and explicable phenomena even to
the most cynical of the so-called scientific minds. It's all a matter of developing powerful enough tools of measurement."

"Does it **flow from human to human?**" I asked, thinking
of my latest kissing bout with Esme Perkins. I'd certainly felt
something akin to an electric charge passing back and forth
between us as we smooched in the woods behind her house,
her mother listening to Nat King Cole in the kitchen not fifty
feet away. But was that love or lust? Or were they both aspects
of the same powerful ray or wave or whatever it was?

"Endlessly and freely," said my uncle, sighing. He was
a handsome man, and exceedingly charming. His lack of a
wife puzzled me. He didn't own a car, spent months at a time

traveling around Europe and Asia, had no visible means of support, and my mother insisted he was a lout, though to me he was a minor god.

"Unless we are afraid," he added suddenly, as if the thought had just occurred to him. Then he smiled at me and sighed again. We sat in silent communion for a piece of time—I'm not sure how long—and I felt comforted for no reason I could name. I felt less confused about my apparent love for Esme, for Celia, for almost every girl I knew who'd deign to speak to me. Something from my uncle, something invisible and as yet undetectable, moved across the space between us and soothed my aching heart.

CHARACTER

"When you wake up in the morning, Pooh," said Piglet at last, "what's the first thing you say to yourself?"

"'What's for breakfast?'" said Pooh. "What do you say, Piglet?"

"I say, 'I wonder what's going to happen exciting today?'" said Piglet.

—A. A. MILNE

W hy do so many of us love *Winnie-the-Pooh* or *The Adventures of Sherlock Holmes* or *Kim* or *To Kill A Mockingbird* or *The Color Purple?* Because we love their characters.

Stories result from the actions of characters. Put an interesting character in a dynamic situation, and you have the makings for a good story. Winnie-the-Pooh, for instance, is a sweet, slow-witted bear who happens to be a slave to honey. Many of the stories that make up the popular classic *Winnie-the-Pooh* spring from Pooh's love of honey and tell how he reacts in his sweet, slow-witted way to the obstacles he encounters while pursuing his favorite food.

In this chapter, we present a series of exercises designed to help you develop your characters and their voices, from which a multitude of stories will spring. You will explore the creation of third-person narrators and discover how their personalities and narrative boundaries set the tone for your stories.

Biography Data Sheets

Much of the raw material for stories comes from your characters' personal histories—how they grew up, where they live, what happened to them in childhood, what they want and love, how they perceive the world. The more you know about your characters, the easier it will be for you to write about them. So let us invent the histories and personality traits of characters by using our Biography Data Sheets.

Basic Exercise
(examples on pages 114–118)

1. Make several copies of the Biography Data Sheet you'll find on the next page.

2. Fill out a data sheet, inventing answers for an imaginary character. You don't need to use complete sentences.

3. Read your data aloud.

4. If you like the character you've created, expand the data, using separate sheets of paper to give you more room for each category.

5. If you don't like the character you've created, or if you only like some of the data, start over with a fresh data sheet.

6. Repeat this process until you get a character you want to explore further.

VARIATION 1. Fill in the data sheet with information from your own life.

VARIATION 2. Fill in the data sheet by mixing fiction with details from your own life.

VARIATION 3. Fill in the data sheet using information from the lives of people you know or have heard about.

VARIATION 4. Create your own version of the Biography Data Sheet, using some or all of our categories and adding new categories that are of particular interest to you. When you have a questionnaire you like, use it to invent a character or characters.

BIOGRAPHY DATA SHEET

Full name:

Age _____ Gender _____ Height _____ Weight _____

Physique, posture, and dress

Occupation/avocations

Where do they live and with whom (include pets)?

How is their abode maintained and decorated?

With whom do they spend their time?

Role in the family as a child/today

A memorable event from childhood

A more recent memorable event

Primary addictions

Recurrent fantasy

What do they love/hate?

Notes:

- Biography Data Sheets can be useful for more fully developing the characters in stories you want to rewrite.
- Some writers like to quickly fill out a Biography Data Sheet (or two) as a warm-up to their writing time.
- If you're writing a play or novel, Biography Data Sheets can help you develop your characters more fully.

For Partners: Cocreate two characters. You will each begin with a blank Biography Data Sheet. Fill out the Ages of your characters and exchange sheets. Fill out the Genders of your characters, and exchange sheets again. Continue exchanging data sheets until the forms are complete.

Use the characters you have created together for Character Explorations (below) or for Dialogue Exercises (page 107). These characters might also be protagonists in stories you write using the techniques in "Arbitrary Story Structures," page 148.

For Groups: Each of you begin a Biography Data Sheet by filling in the Age category. Now pass your sheets to the left. Fill in the Gender category, then pass the sheets to the left again. Continue this process until your composite characters are complete. Read the data sheets aloud. Assign a cocreated character to each member of the group and use them for Character Explorations (below) and Dialogue Exercises (page 107).

Character Explorations

Having completed a Biography Data Sheet (page 101) you're happy with, you now have the profile of a character. Here are a number of exercises that will help deepen and clarify your vision of your character. Read over your data sheet before you begin each exercise. Try to write a half-page or more for each exploration you attempt. You may use first, second, or third person and any tense you choose for these explorations.

- Describe your character's face and body.

- Have your character describe her/his own face and body.

- Have your character talk about her/his most memorable teacher (example on page 119).

- Describe your character (or some aspect of them) in her/his mother's voice (example on page 120).

- Have your character talk about her/his mother.

- Describe your character (or some aspect of them) in her/his father's voice.

- Have your character talk about her/his father.

- Have one of your character's teachers (past or present) talk about your character.

- Have your character write a letter to a friend about a recent experience or dream.

- Have your character speak about her/his favorite food.

- Have your character speak about an early sensual memory.

- Have your character speak about darkness.

- Interview your character (example on page 121).

- Assume the personality of your character and do some of the other exercises in this book.

- Make your character the protagonist of an Arbitrary Story Structure (page 148).

- Describe in detail a memorable event from your character's childhood (example on page 122).

- Have your character describe her/his vision of the future.

- Write a dialogue between your character and her/his best friend.

- Describe your character partaking of one or more of her/his primary addictions (example on page 124).

- Describe your character waking up and getting dressed.

- Describe your character's home.

OUR BLISS

Writing about the joys of childhood can be a great way to access characters and stories while developing positive feelings about the writing process.

Basic Exercise

(examples on pages 125–126)

1. Close your eyes and relax for a moment, allowing yourself to remember happy moments from your childhood. What images come to mind? Try to remember what game or pastime you loved more than any other.

2. Take a few minutes to write a description of this pleasurable experience. Read aloud.

3. Take a few more minutes to write about this experience as if you are involved in it now, using first person, present tense; for example:

I am sitting in the backyard making mud pies.

Read aloud.

4. Now describe this activity again, as if you are observing yourself, using third person, present tense; for example:

Tommy sits on a high stool at the kitchen table watching his grandmother make the dough for chocolate chip cookies.

Read aloud.

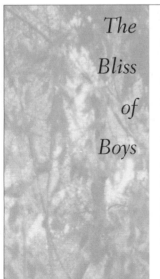

The Bliss of Boys

"Don't be surprised if only a few of the boys participate. Most of them *hate* writing. Unless their grade depends on it, they don't do anything."

These words of warning preceded my appearance before thirty stone-faced sixteen-year-old boys. The atmosphere in that college prep classroom was rife with stress and fear of failure. Not a happy bunch.

I read a short story that seemed to animate a few faces. Then I said, "Here is my question to you. What was it you did when you were a little boy—five or six—that was transcendent of time? By transcendent of time, I mean the experience of *no* time, endless time, bliss, when you and what you were doing were indistinguishable. I want you to take a few minutes to write about this memory of your bliss. No one else need hear or see what you write, unless you want to share it. Go."

Every boy in the class, without hesitation, began to write furiously. When I called time after ten minutes, all of the boys continued writing. Their teacher was flabbergasted, and we didn't have time to hear the memories of all who volunteered to read aloud. ⌇TW

VARIATION 1. Repeat the exercise using your memories of a friend or acquaintance as inspiration.

VARIATION 2. Repeat the exercise using your parent or parents (or another influential adult) as the main character for this exercise.

For Partners: After sharing what you've written, talk about your memories, asking each other questions to elicit more details. Now write about your bliss again.

For Groups: Listen carefully to each person's memory, then jot down on a sheet of paper or index card the first question that comes to your mind. Pass these questions to the reader. When everyone has their questions, repeat any or all of the steps of the basic exercise, attempting in the process to answer the questions posed.

Another way for a group to make use of pleasurable memories is to choose a few general topics—food, vacations, sensuality—and take turns talking about happy memories connected to these things. If any topic seems particularly inspiring to the group, do some free-writing about it.

Writing

Pleasure

Memory is magical. Research has shown that calling to mind a happy memory, or even having a fantasy about something wonderful, can lower blood pressure and relieve pain. Memories of pleasurable experiences can evoke a profound peacefulness in body and mind. Out of this peaceful state flows writing that feels effortless.

Pleasurable memory exercises like "Our Bliss" provide a soothing break from more difficult writing practice. Whenever you're feeling anxious or angry or depressed, remember your good times and write about them in all their glorious detail.

If you can't think of a single happy memory, make something up. Live it in your mind as if it were real. There's no law against inventing a happy childhood event or a perfect love affair, and there may be tremendous psychological and physiological benefit in doing so.✒︎MT

OUR FEARS

While contemplating our bliss may unleash a torrent of effortless writing, examining our fears can prove a more challenging exercise. Though we are often reluctant to look deeply at uncomfortable emotions, but keep in mind that the process of exploring the shadowy parts of ourselves brings emotional power and depth to our writing. Allow plenty of time. For most people, this exercise could easily generate an entire day of writing.

*Basic
Exercise*
(example on page 127)

1. Take a moment to ground yourself, feeling the steadfast support of the earth beneath you. Breathe a few deep breaths, inhaling into your belly and exhaling slowly. Let this be a time of looking inward with compassion, bringing buried information up to the light.

2. At the top of the page, write "What am I afraid of?" then quickly jot down the first five answers that come to mind.

3. Choose one of your answers and write it at the top of a blank page.

4. Now write down everything that occurs to you about this fear: its color and shape, how it feels in your body, where it originated and how long it has been with you, what triggers it.

5. Write a positively worded statement in the present tense—an affirmation—about what you wish for in regard to this fear. If your fear is of heights, for instance, you might write the affirmation: "I FEEL SAFE AND SECURE EVERYWHERE, EVEN AT GREAT HEIGHTS."

6. Read the piece aloud, then go on to another fear on your list and repeat the process.

For Partners: Each of you select a fear using steps 1, 2, and 3 above, then share your lists and tell each other which fear you have chosen to work with. For a new step 4, take turns coming up with six to eight questions you will both use to examine your fears. For a new step 5, use these questions to prompt a page of writing about your fear (you don't have to answer all the questions). You may choose not to read your finished piece aloud, though it can be very therapeutic to admit your fears openly and it will increase the trust between you.

For Groups: Make this a fiction-writing exercise by selecting something unusual to use as the object of fear (for example, a merry-go-round), then have everyone in the group do the basic exercise as if they were actually afraid of the selected object.

DIALOGUE EXERCISES

Every writer has her own notion of how dialogue should sound. But whatever your notions about dialogue, it is essential that you read aloud any dialogue you have written to hear how it sounds as conversation. What we may hear in our heads is not always what we hear when we read dialogue aloud. We may think in silence, but we talk out loud.

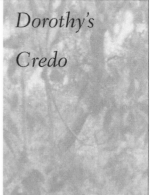

Dorothy's Credo

My first literary agent—the late, great Dorothy Pittman—had two fundamental rules for writing dialogue. These rules applied to novels, short stories, plays, and screenplays.

1. Don't preach.
2. Stay in character.

Though I subscribe to no set rules for how to write, I repeat Dorothy's directives as food for thought about writing strong, appealing dialogue.༃TW

Classic Situations

Basic Exercise

(examples on pages 129–130)

1. Think of a classic dialogue situation, or choose one from the following list.

   - Teen coming home late caught by parent

   - Couple breaking up

   - Boss firing employee

   - Policeman interrogating suspect

   - Someone lost asking for directions

2. List five characteristics for each of the characters involved, or fill out a Biography Data Sheet (page 101) for each character.

3. Set the scene with a descriptive paragraph. For example:

   Mary, a petite woman of forty, is sitting on the sofa in her living room waiting for John, her boyfriend of seven years. For the first time in their relationship, John, a nervous man of fifty, comes in without knocking.

4. Write the dialogue.

5. Read your scene aloud, then make any changes you like.

VARIATION 1. Using the same classic situation, change the personality/biography data of one of your characters, and write the scene again.

VARIATION 2. Using the same situation, change the personalities/biography data of both characters, and write the scene again.

VARIATION 3. Using the same situation and characters, write two or three dialogues in different styles (for example, comic, tragic, melodramatic, modern, Shakespearean).

For Partners: Each of you take the role of one of the characters, then verbally improvise the scene a few times. When you think you've got a good feel for the character dynamics, each of you write a version of the scene.

Classic Topics

1. Choose a topic from the following list.

   * What do you really want to be?

   * Where would you ideally like to live?

   * Sex

   * Love

   * Marriage

   * Death

   * Fate

2. Invent two characters, either by filling out two Biography Data Sheets (page 101) or by listing five traits for each character.

3. Set the scene with a descriptive paragraph; for example:

   Bobby, seventeen, and Susie, fifteen, meet in the park at sunset to flirt. Susie wants to keep the relationship flirtatious, with the occasional kiss, but Bobby is eager to take things beyond kissing.

4. Write the dialogue.

5. Read your scene aloud, then make any changes you like.

VARIATION 1. Using the same characters, change the topic and write the scene again.

VARIATION 2. Using the same topic, change the personality/biography data of one of your characters, and write the scene again.

VARIATION 3. Using the same situation and characters, write two or three dialogues in different styles (for example, comic, tragic, melodramatic, modern, Shakespearean).

For Partners: Each of you take the role of one of the characters, then verbally improvise the scene together a few times. When you think you've got a good feel for the character

When we read our words to another person, we often hear them more clearly. Knowing our writing is being heard by another sharpens our self-perception.

dynamics, use Partner Writing (page 25) to cowrite two versions of the scene.

The Modified Interview

Interviews are a form of dialogue, though usually the person being interviewed does more of the talking. There is, however, a way to modify the interview form to make a more balanced dialogue.

1. Create two characters.

2. Have Character #1 ask a question of Character #2.

3. Have Character #2 reply to the question, ending her reply with a question for Character #1.

4. Have Character #1 reply to Character #2's question, ending her reply with a question, and so forth.

5. When each character has answered and asked five questions, read your interview aloud.

6. Write a scene in third person involving your two characters. Use parts of your interview, including questions, to create the dialogue for your scene.

For Partners: Use Partner Writing to create two interviews simultaneously, then complete step 6 individually.

INTERVIEW TO CREATE CHARACTER

The interview can be an effective way to invent a character's personality by writing his or her responses to questions. (Our Basic Interview Process is described on page 32; an example of an interview used to create character can be found on page 133.)

Here are twenty-four questions, some of which you might find useful for generating details of your character's personality and lifestyle.

- Where were you born?

- Do you believe in astrology?

- What do you believe in?

- How do you feel, in general, about the opposite sex?

- What are you obsessed with?

- What is your favorite music?

- When are you most content?

- How do you feel about forgiveness?

- Is sex important to you? Why?

- Your house is burning. You can save only one book. Which will it be?

- Tell us about your mother/father.

- Did you, or do you, enjoy school?

- Is there justice in the world?

- Do you have theories about things?

- What do you want for your birthday?

- Have you ever had a mystical experience?

- Do you believe humans are superior to animals?

- Do you ever give money to beggars?

- Are you an expert at anything?

- What did you (do you) want to be when you grew (grow) up?

- Are you satisfied with your body?

- Describe your ideal friend.

- What do you want to be remembered for?

- Any words of wisdom you'd like to share?

Narrative Boundaries

An effective third-person narrator has consistent narrative boundaries and a distinct personality—which may or may not be the personality of the author. To better understand the effects of narrative boundaries, study a few of your favorite books written in third person. Note the traits and limitations of each narrator. What do you like about each voice? Can you describe the personalities of the narrators? What do they choose to reveal about their various characters? What do they not reveal? All these factors contribute to the unique tone and perspective of the book.

Experimenting with Narrative Boundaries

Basic Exercise
(example on page 134)

1. Think about what kind of narrator you want for your story. You may complete a Biography Data Sheet (page 101) to help you invent a persona you'll enjoy working with.

2. Create a list of traits and limitations for your narrator. The list might look something like this:

   * British

   * Erudite; complex sentences

   * Knows the life histories of all his characters

   * Doesn't know what his characters are thinking, but does know how they feel about things

   * Prefers women to men

   * Loves the expression, *Be that as it may*

   * Likes dialogue that seems unconnected to the story he's telling

3. Write a rough draft of a third-person short story in the voice of this narrator. You might want to use an Arbitrary Story Structure (page 148) to help you craft the first draft.

4. Modify your original list of traits and limitations to give your narrator a different perspective. For example, the list above could be modified in the following way:

- Jewish

- Erudite; complex sentences

- Knows the life histories of all his characters

- Knows what his characters are thinking

- Doesn't like women

- Loves the word *nevertheless*

- All dialogues are arguments

5. Rewrite the story using your modified list.

VARIATION 1. Make a list of traits and limitations about yourself.

VARIATION 2. Make your initial list of traits and limitations similar to those you find in a favorite book or story.

BIOGRAPHY DATA SHEET
(see page 119)

Full name: **Grace Alexander**

Age **62** Gender **F** Height **5'10"** Weight **160**

Physique, posture, and dress
Erect and elegant in slate gray tunic and slacks

Occupation/avocations
CEO of Ah! Roma perfumes and herbal cosmetics.
Plays cello. Regularly attends meditation retreats.

Where do they live and with whom (include pets)?
A stone villa in Tuscany set in an old vineyard.
Lives with 4 other creatively accomplished women/
9 cats

How is their abode maintained and decorated?
Meticulous order. Rennaisance art; Buddhist
statuary; lush Turkish carpets on floors & walls.

With whom do they spend their time?
Opera singers, sculptors and painters, poets and
musicians; contemplatives of every stripe.

Role in the family as a child/today
Eldest; 4 younger brothers; family trailblazer;
serious student. Today, she's adored by three
surviving brothers.

A memorable event from childhood
Swam freestyle in Olympics—bronze medal.

A more recent memorable event
On 60th birthday, traversed the European
continent by hot air balloon.

Primary addictions
Espresso and fresh flowers in every room.

Recurrent fantasy
Creating an artist's colony/temple to nurture
creative and spiritual freedom.

What do they love/hate?
Loves animated discussions on art, spirit, life.
Hates arrogant academics.

BIOGRAPHY DATA SHEET

(see page 120)

Full name: **Frances Fleming**

Age **49**   Gender **F**   Height **5'10"**   Weight **125**

Physique, posture, and dress

Angular, dramatic features, large hips for one so thin
Modigliani face, youthful yet sad, pants not dresses, short hair

Occupation/avocations

Biographer of women scientists; writes entries for
encyclopedias; birdwatcher, backpacker, film buff.

Where do they live and with whom (include pets)?

An apartment with view of Lake Merritt in Oakland CA. Building is an
architectural landmark (1920) Two dogs: Mutt and Jeff

How is their abode maintained and decorated?

Soft, comfy furniture in deep colors; some nice oak
antiques; black & white photos on display. Neat, but not
compulsive.

With whom do they spend their time?

Landlord Melvin Thoms is her favorite birding companion. Nieces and nephews drop
by to play with telescopes, microscopes, other groovy tools. Members of long-standing
women's support group

Role in the family as a child/today

Has twin brother, younger sister. Always the studious
outdoor type, shy with some people. Today, she is super-
auntie.

A memorable event from childhood

Read a little blue book about Amelia Earhart, became so excited couldn't sleep
for three days! Never had occurred to her that women could be heroes.

A more recent memorable event

Sea-kayaking trip off coast of British Columbia.
Humpback whales swam beside her.

Primary addictions

Fine port, original black and white photography (apartment sports dozens of
framed prints, including two Dorothea Langes.)

Recurrent fantasy

To discover an unsung woman scientist whose
important work she successfully champions.

What do they love/hate?

love: old romantic movies (Casablanca), her dogs, friends, Nature, the ocean
hate: sexism, lumber companies, how swiftly time passes

BIOGRAPHY DATA SHEET

(see page 121)

Full name: Dawn Marie Carter

Age 37 Gender F Height 5'9" Weight 142

Physique, posture, and dress

A dancer/athlete: muscular, stands on toes, sweat pants sleeveless shirts, no bra

Occupation/avocations

massage therapist - women only   Gambling - cards

Where do they live and with whom (include pets)?

a trailer in South Lake Tahoe - summers
winter: share apartment in Venice Beach, CA. / chaco - cockatiel
                                                Benny - small mutt

How is their abode maintained and decorated?

Trailer dominated by bed and massage table - Posters of Buddhist nuns, clean,
Venice Beach ~ massage table in campy household   incense, fresh flowers

With whom do they spend their time?

other women athletes, artists, Buddhists, dog owners, gamblers,
    lesbians, family

Role in the family as a child/today

oldest child, father absent, mom dating / Beloved aunt to her brothers'
    acted as parent to younger brothers / children, estranged from her mother

A memorable event from childhood

when she was nine, being left alone for a week to care for her
    younger brothers - many adventures therein

A more recent memorable event

While playing frisbee on the beach with Benny, saw an Orca (killer whale)
    swimming alongside a wind surfer

Primary addictions

Gambling, romance

Recurrent fantasy

To meet a man who turns her on as much as women do, and
    to have a child with him

What do they love/hate?

Love: Buddhist Koans, puppies, Benny,   Hate: Destruction of the environment,
chaco, nieces, nephews, winning   cruelty to animals, thoughtless
                                                            parents

BIOGRAPHY DATA SHEET

(see page 122)

Full name: *Alexander Cesar Cedeño*

Age _*55*_ Gender _*M*_ Height _*5'9"*_ Weight _*198*_

Physique, posture, and dress
> *Bull of a man, slight forward hunch, aggressive, comfortable old clothes, pendleton shirts, berets*

Occupation/avocations
> *Professor of Philosophy, University of California, Santa Cruz*

Where do they live and with whom (include pets)?
> *Santa Cruz mountains, small house in redwood glade, with wife Irenia, 52 old golden retriever - Hegel - and a parrot named Wittgenstein*

How is their abode maintained and decorated?
> *Sparse, funky, thousands of books, cozy, woodstove, bird feeders out every window, large abstract paintings, Persian rugs*

With whom do they spend their time?
> *Irenia, musicians, students, philosophers, neighbors, fishermen*

Role in the family as a child/today
> *Oldest son of six children, was supposed to become a priest, hyper-responsible until twelve, then rebelled. Today, one of four surviving children, siblings all live in Spain. He is close to one nephew.*

A memorable event from childhood
> *seven: got lost in woods, guided to safety by a translucent being he believes was an angel*

A more recent memorable event
> *while lecturing on the philosophical underpinnings of psychosis, saw halos over heads of several people in the audience*

Primary addictions
> *cigars, women, being right, red wine*

Recurrent fantasy
> *Becomes lovers with French movie actress, has three children with her*

What do they love/hate?
> *love: American college students trying to elucidate complex ideas, French movies, walking, sex, Irenia   hate: fascism, corporate greed, aging*

BIOGRAPHY DATA SHEET
(see page 124)

Full name: **Paul Clayton**

Age **14**   Gender **M**   Height **5'6"**   Weight **110**

Physique, posture, and dress
Erect, but slumps around friends, wiry frame. Likes old comfy clothes,
    crazy for basketball shoes

Occupation/avocations
Summer job picking fruit w/cousins in the Imperial
Valley. Catches adventure movies on opening weekend.
                                        Builds model cars.

Where do they live and with whom (include pets)?
 Visalia, Calif in an older tract home - has his own room.   Mother: Elaine 40
Father- Biff 35   sister Kaitlin 16   Brother Rafe 11   Black Lab- Congo   Cat- Duffy

How is their abode maintained and decorated?
Home is conventional middle America suburban style.
His room: posters of super models & stock cars, black light.

With whom do they spend their time?
  Best friend Franco - 15 - more worldly. They go to the race track (cars), smoke clove cigs,
    talk about sex (with girls)

Role in the family as a child/today
Middle child; mother's ally against wild father; idol of
younger brother; hated by sister; evades most confront-
                                        ations with dad.

A memorable event from childhood
   seven: he and his sister rode air mattresses for several miles in an irrigation
     ditch - rescued by fire department, though they were in no danger

A more recent memorable event
Won a free throw basketball contest at his high
school; afterwards, was kissed by cheerleader.

Primary addictions
   coffee drinks, chocolate, movies

Recurrent fantasy
Elle McPherson moves in next door and frequently
sunbathes nude on the back deck.

What do they love/hate?
  love gross noises Franco makes with his armpit, cars, sports, & certain pom pom girl
  hate father, school, older guys on the football team with pom pom girl girlfriends

Character Explorations—*Have your character talk about her/his most memorable teacher, page 102 (MT)*

GRACE ALEXANDER
(see page 114 for her Biography Data Sheet)

I recall, quite vividly, my humanities instructor in high school—Paula Fabiani. She was well-built but not tall and wore her hair in a style quite short by the standards of the day, yet on her it looked pretty and feminine. She always seemed to be bristling with a kind of electricity, so strong was the life force in her. She looked everyone directly in the eye and spoke with great caring and conviction. I thought she was the perfect person, a professional woman who defied social expectations yet thoroughly enjoyed people. I heard much later that she had moved on to teaching at the university. She never married, explaining without apology that she preferred the nurturing company of women to the demanding company of men.

Ms. Fabiani was born and reared in Rome until age eleven, when one of Italy's constant political turnabouts put her father—a well-known leftist journalist—in danger. The rest of her childhood was spent in rural Wisconsin, but she made frequent trips back to Italy, which was, she often reminded us, her *spiritual* home. She loved Renaissance art and music and architecture with great passion and spoke ecstatically of the museums of Europe.

At age sixteen, sitting in Ms. Fabiani's classroom on a chilly autumn day listening to her stirring lecture on the life of da Vinci, I decided without a doubt that I would someday live in Rome and immerse myself in the world's most sensual yet exalted culture. And though I found Rome too crowded, too noisy, for lengthy residence, Italy has become my spiritual home, as well.

Ms. Fabiani, with her enthusiasm and acute sensibilities and extraordinary independence, gave me my life, really, my wonderful life, and I shall always be grateful to her.

Examples

of

Character

Exercises

Character Explorations—*Describe your character (or some aspect of them) in her/his mother's voice, Partner Writing, page 102 (TW/MT) [Slashes provided to demonstrate three-line exchange process.]*

FRANCES FLEMING

(see page 115 for her Biography Data Sheet)

She's always been thin, but on her it looks good, elegant, I think. I am proud of Frances, but more importantly, I *enjoy* her. \\ What a mind! Sometimes I'll be listening to her and I'll think, *Where did she get this big intellect? Certainly not from her father. Could it be from me?* \\ I admit I envy Frances. Her life is so much her *own*, something a woman doesn't experience if she chooses to have children. \\

I'll never forget the night she read that little biography of Amelia Earhart. She was eight. I was making her lunch for school the next \\ day, and she came running into the kitchen and looked at me so strangely I thought she was ill. "Can we get an airplane?" she \\ asked, her eyes as big as plates. "You can learn to fly, and I'll be your copilot until I'm bigger, and we'll go so far and…" And then she started gasping \\ and I made her sit down and take small sips of water until she was calmer. "No airplanes in the budget this month," \\ I said, making light of what I soon realized was a huge explosion of everything she'd ever believed girls could do with their lives.

She looked up from her glass of water. I can still see the wonder, the fear, the *change* in her, as if her face had expanded in a matter of moments. Then she said, "Okay, but we can get more books, okay? About ladies like her."

"Of course," I said, though at the time I couldn't imagine where we'd *find* them.

Character Explorations—*Interview your character, page 102. (TW)*

DAWN MARIE CARTER
(see page 116 for her Biography Data Sheet)

TODD: When did you become interested in gambling?

DAWN: Honey, my whole life has been one big gamble. *(laughter)* Actually, my mother was a cocktail waitress in a casino. She taught us how to play blackjack and poker before we could talk. My brothers and I played cards all the time when we weren't playing ball or watching television. And when my mom was home, we played cards with her. It just kind of went from there.

TODD: When was your first big win?

DAWN: Oh, I remember that vividly. The night of the junior prom. After the dance, I went with my date to a party at the house of the richest kid at our school.

TODD: Where was this?

DAWN: Reno. A snowy night. But the pool was heated and his parents were out of town, so there was lots of naked kids in the pool, and drinking and pot smoking. But I wasn't interested in that. I wanted in on the poker game upstairs in the card room. This was like a major mansion, and these boys were seriously into acting like gangsters. They were smoking cigars, and had their cutie-pies bringing them drinks. They didn't want to let me play at first, but I kept after them, and they let me in. I was pretty cute back then myself, and I think that helped the cause. We played until five in the morning. I won three thousand dollars. After that, I was hooked.

TODD: When did you become a Buddhist?

DAWN: I don't call myself a Buddhist. I love reading Buddhist texts, and I meditate, but I don't have a formal practice. The ideas come closest to my own way of thinking.

TODD: How do Buddhist beliefs and gambling go together?

DAWN: You know, the thing is, people who don't know any better assume all gamblers have a gambling problem. I can
hear you thinking that by the tone of your voice. But I don't
have a problem. It's the way I make part of my income.
Some people play the stock market. Some people gamble
on starting a business. You gamble on the publishing indus-
try liking what you write. I gamble with cards. I have a
highly refined set of skills. If I get into a game and I intuit
I'm out of my league, I get out of the game. A gambler with
a problem stays in. You see the difference?

TODD: So a Buddhist practice supports your gambling practice.

DAWN: I guess it does. Learning to be absolutely present, undis-
tracted by the past or the future, has definitely improved
my playing. I think because it sharpens my intuition.

TODD: And frisbee. You're somewhat famous on Venice Beach
for your frisbee stunts with your dog Benny.

DAWN: Oh, yeah. We love showing off, and the summer wind
off Venice Beach can be so dreamy perfect sometimes, it's
like dancing with God.

Character Explorations—*Describe in detail a memorable
event from your character's childhood, page 102 (TW)*

ALEXANDER CESAR CEDEÑO
(see page 117 for his Biography Data Sheet)

I have to laugh at myself. I've met disembodied spirits
dozens of times in my life, yet I worry about the stock market. I
owe my life to the intervention of angels, yet I bristle at the
word "angel." My life is concrete proof of the wildest notions of
metaphysics, yet I mock my students who believe in the occult.

When I was a boy in Spain, seven, eight years old, my
mother would lend me to her maiden aunt for weeks at a time
so the dear woman wouldn't be so lonely. I liked going to Tia.
She lived in the country in a big house in which I had my own
room, a luxury I didn't have at home. She was a fine cook, and

she loved nothing so much as stuffing me with cookies and cake. I remember, too, she roasted chickens on a spit in her fireplace. My God, they melted in your mouth.

In the evenings she would read to me, and she taught me songs, too. During the day I was free for hours at a time while she tended her bees and chickens and vegetable garden. So I played in the woods, pretending I was an explorer in the New World, fighting Indians and discovering gold. Or I would hide behind a tree and wait for the forest animals to show themselves. I saw rabbits and deer, and once I saw a large, silver fox. Tia insisted only that I stay within earshot of her, and come when she called.

One day, however, I broke her rule and wandered a long way from home. I didn't do this consciously. I was lost in a game of exploration, and the game became so real I forgot about my other reality. When I came to my senses, I found myself on the banks of a swiftly flowing stream in a part of the forest I had not experienced—a wild place with enormous trees and huge boulders that looked like the heads of giants.

I had no idea in which direction Tia's house lay and the day was drawing to a close. So I did what my mother told me to do when I needed help. I bowed my head and prayed. I even remember my prayer. "Please God, help me find my way home so Tia will not be upset. She suffers terrible indigestion when she worries."

I opened my eyes, and there on the other side of the stream was what appeared to be a naked boy, but he wasn't only naked, he was translucent—like pinkish quartz—and his eyes were black beads. He beckoned to me, and because I believed him to be the answer to my prayer, I bravely jumped from stone to stone and crossed the torrent.

I followed this fantastic apparition into the woods, the darkness closing around us. But I was not afraid. My guide seemed to glow from within, so even when it grew almost pitch black I was able to see him.

After a long time we came out of the dense forest and entered a grove of stately oaks, and these gave way to an orchard of apple trees. I knew those trees! They were Tia's.

"Tia! Tia!" I cried, seeing her house in the distance.

Examples

of

Character

Exercises

Then I realized my guide was gone, though he had just been a few paces ahead of me. I ran to the house. Tia was in her kitchen, kneading dough for the evening's bread.

"I was just about to call you," she said as I came into the room. "Where have you been?"

"In the forest," I said, trembling all over from my adventure. "Following a spirit. An angel, I think."

"The forest is full of angels," she said, smiling at me. "But be careful, hijo. There are devils, too, and they sometimes look for all the world like angels."

Character Explorations—*Describe your character partaking of one or more of her/his primary addictions, page 102 (TW)*

PAUL CLAYTON
(see page 118 for his Biography Data Sheet)

Last weekend my mom and dad and Kaitlin and Rafe all went to Disneyland. I couldn't go because I had a track meet Saturday morning, so I got to stay home alone overnight for the first time in my life. Well, I wasn't completely alone because I had Congo, my dog, and Duffy, our cat, but I was the only human.

Franco, he's my best friend, wanted to have a big party here, but if my dad found out he'd murder me, so instead we rode our bikes downtown and got six triple espressos to go from Java City, picked up a large fudge brownie cake at Just Desserts, and rented our three favorite movies, *The Breakfast Club, Reality Bites,* and *Pump Up the Volume.* When we got home we ordered an extra-large pepperoni pizza delivered from Domino's.

Our plan was to scarf the pizza, and then drink an espresso each for each movie. We'd eat a third of the cake for each film. Pace ourselves and stay high. We started with *Reality Bites.* We each had an espresso and a sixth of the cake, but then we both got so horny watching Winona Ryder, we dared each other to call girls, and Franco actually did. He called Carla Carpenter. I was supposed to call Renee Fernandez, not that I ever would have, but she was *with* Carla, and Franco talked them both into coming over. I don't know how he did it, but he did.

I was stoked but totally nervous. Renee Fernandez is this amazing chicana pom pom girl. When I won the free throw shooting contest a couple months ago, I won a kiss from her and I practically fainted when she kissed me. She's sixteen and awesomely cute, with a body you can hardly believe. Carla is fifteen. Franco is fifteen. I'm only fourteen, but I'll be fifteen in two weeks, and I look older. Anyway, it seemed impossible they were coming over. I thought maybe Franco was just bluffing, but then the doorbell rang and there they were.

We split the espressos with them and watched *The Breakfast Club*. I watched Renee more than I watched the movie. I mean, here she actually was, on the sofa about four feet away from me, and every once in a while she'd smile at me, and I'd about die.

Our Bliss—*Basic Exercise, page 103 (MT)*

BASIC MEMORY:

Living on the edge of a small town was heaven for me as a kid. Within easy rambling distance were small farms with their horses and barns and flowerbeds. A favorite destination for my adventuring was a huge boulder that sat beside a miniature creek. To reach it, I had to follow deer tracks through thick riparian brush, sometimes crawling on my belly. The smells and sounds enveloped me and I felt my animal nature more purely then—at seven or eight—than ever before or since.

FIRST PERSON:

This deep, round hole in the rock is the place where Indian women ground corn and acorns for the daily meal. My brother, Will, says so, and I know it's true because I can *feel* these women crouching beside me, hear their storytelling and songs. The pocket of my dungarees is full of arrowheads, bits of moss, and strange seedpods I will ask Will about when I get home. This is my first solo visit to my favorite boulder. I crawled on my belly to reach it and my arms and face are scratched up. I'm sweaty and dirty, but I've never felt so happy, so at home in the world. So myself.

THIRD PERSON:

The raggedy girl crouches alone on top of the creek's biggest boulder. It's hard to imagine how she found this place, how she managed to scale the twenty-foot boulder to the ancient grinding holes that attract archeologists from all over the state. She is quite still, staring down into the stone, only occasionally poking at it with a stick she has broken off of a dead branch overhead. On her face is a mixture of puzzlement and peace, like she's trying to figure something out and knows she eventually will. She stretches out on her back, staring up at the sky, and points upward, drawing with her finger the outlines of clouds as they drift by. The sun has begun to drop behind the ridge to the west before she picks herself up and heads home.

Our Bliss—*Basic Exercise, page 104 (TW)*

BASIC MEMORY:

I loved to fish. I can see the clear water of the Tuolumne where it flowed through Tuolumne Meadows. We camped there for several summers and I fished for the better part of every day. I had a little spinning rod and reel and my very own creel, just like my dad's. The sky there was so blue, the air so clean, the river so full of promise. Sometimes I'd fish close to our camp. Other times I'd walk downstream to a deep pool where I could see the trout finning against the current. My heart would pound and I'd kneel down in the deep grass to bait my hook. Then I'd stand up, cast my worm or fly into the stream, and pray for a fish to strike.

FIRST PERSON:

I grab my pole and my creel and run down to the river. Mom calls after me, "Be careful." I wish I'd started earlier. The fish always bite better early in the morning. I run along the little trail through high grass, my shoes and pants getting wet from the dew. But I don't care because I'll dry off in the sun as I fish. I woke up before dawn today thinking about the big fish I saw in the pool below the rock where Dad likes to dive in. I want to fish there today before anybody goes swimming and scares the fish away. When I get close to the pool, I slow down.

My heart is pounding. I'm sure I'll catch that big trout. If I can just get my worm in the water without startling him, he'll take it. I know he will.

THIRD PERSON:

The boy is seven or eight. He has a look of intense concentration on his face. His jacket and jeans are soiled from days of camping, but his face is clean. He is standing beside a swiftly flowing river—the Tuolumne—where it spills over an enormous gray rock and drops down into a deep pool. He has a fishing pole, its line baited with a big worm. He stares at the pool, then prepares to cast his line into the pool. His every cell seems concentrated on the effort of throwing the worm to the very base of the waterfall. He carefully brings the pole back over his head, checks the worm, checks the pool once more, and makes his cast. He is so happy with his cast, he jumps with pleasure, and gives a cry of triumph.

Our Fears—*Partner Exercise, page 106 (TW/MT)*

2 and 3: Individual lists of fears; one fear selected.

> MINDY'S LIST: *"What am I afraid of?"* (selected fear in caps)
> 1. FLYING IN AIRPLANES
> 2. Being old and alone
> 3. Disability
> 4. Nuclear winter
> 5. Death of my loved ones

4. Taking turns, create a list of questions to use in examining the fears.

   * How would your life be different if you didn't have this fear?

   * Where do you think this fear comes from?

   * How often do you feel this fear?

   * Do you ever dream about the thing you fear happening?

   * What color is the fear?

   * Have you tried to overcome this fear?

Examples

of

Character

Exercises

- Is there anyone who you don't want to know about this fear?

- Is there another fear connected to this fear?

5. Use the questions to prompt a page of writing.

FEAR OF FLYING (MT)

In December of 1980, within a month of my father's death from stroke complications, my friend Dan Martinez died in a DC-10 crash in Mexico City. Dan was a good man, he was honest and loving, he was a spiritual being well ahead of me on the path.

Up to this point I had enjoyed flying, had found it exhilarating, had considered myself invulnerable. After Dan's accident I spent obsessive hours imagining his final moments. This scared me silly and I still go into physical panic at the prospect of flying, though I have taken a few short trips since then without dying, either of fright or in a fiery crash.

If I didn't have this fear I would have spent more time in Hawaii, would have explored the Southwest and Canada and the Yucatan and Europe. On the upside, perhaps this fear has served me by requiring that I stay put more than my gypsy nature might otherwise dictate— "bloom where you're planted" and all that.

This last comment is nonsense, I realize as I write it. In fact, I am certain that being locked inside a heavy steel contraption that burns up vast quantities of nonrenewable fossil fuel to travel at breathtaking speed thousands of miles above the earth could only enhance my life.

This fear is some dark, deep color, but it is not solid. Sometimes, when I'm feeling really together, healthy and creative and spiritually attuned, I can contemplate plane trips without my chest getting choked with fear. A woman once gave me a pill that made a flight from Seattle to Sacramento a truly lovely experience. I should have learned the name of that happy-making drug.

Dialogue Exercise—*Classic Situations, Basic Exercise combined with Variation 3, page 108 (TW)*

1. Situation chosen from list: *Boss firing employee*

2. List five characteristics for each of the characters involved.
   Boss: *middle-aged, male, tired, unhappy, alcoholic*
   EMPLOYEE: *young, female, angry, frightened, lonely*

3. Set the scene with a descriptive paragraph.

   Bernie, a heavy set man of fifty-three, is sitting at his desk in his cluttered office at Amalgamated Stuff, where he's worked for twenty-two years. Tiffany, twenty-three, her makeup smeared from crying, knocks tentatively on Bernie's open door.

4. The dialogue.

   BERNIE: (*Stands with some effort*) Come in, Tiffany. Come in. Have a seat.

   TIFFANY: (*Enters painfully, remains standing*) I can explain everything.

   BERNIE: Sit. Please.

   TIFFANY: (*Looks around*) Where?

   BERNIE: (*Realizes the two chairs are full of stuff, gets up*) Sorry. (*Moves stuff off one chair onto the floor*) Here.

   TIFFANY: Thank you. (*Looks around*) You know, I could help you clean up your office if you'd like.

   BERNIE: (*Sitting down heavily*) Tiffany, look. I like you. You're a bright, energetic—

   TIFFANY: But I'm fired.

   BERNIE: I'm afraid so.

   TIFFANY: What are *you* afraid of? You've got a job, and health insurance, and a house, and retirement. I've got nothing.

   BERNIE: Sorry. It was a figure of speech.

TIFFANY: Yeah, right. It's so unfair. You didn't even let me explain.

BERNIE: So explain.

TIFFANY: Why bother? You won't believe me anyway.

BERNIE: I might. (*Looks at his watch*) Go ahead.

TIFFANY: You timing this?

BERNIE: (*Breaking*) Look, I don't have to put up with this crap from you. We've lost at least three customers because of your screw-ups, and now you're giving me attitude?

TIFFANY: I'm sorry. I just—I'm in trouble, okay? I need this job. Or some job. So maybe I'm not so great with numbers. But I'm a good organizer. You should see my apartment. You want to see my apartment, Bernie? I'll fix us a little dinner. We'll have a little wine. What do you say?

BERNIE: Sorry, honey. Ten years ago, maybe. But not tonight.

TIFFANY: (*Stands*) Can I ask you a favor?

BERNIE: What?

TIFFANY: Can you just say I wasn't right for the job, and not that I messed up?

BERNIE: Sure. I can do that. That I can do.

Dialogue Exercise—*A second version (TW)*

Using the same situation and characters, write a dialogue in a wholly different style: Shakespearean.

The tower of London. Bernard, a gentleman, sits at his desk. Enter Tiffania, a fair lass.

TIFFANIA: You summoned me, my lord?

BERNARD: (*Stands with some effort*) Sit thyself by the fire, Tiffania. The day is bitter cold.

TIFFANIA: (*Remains standing*) The day may be bitter, but sweet next to my misery, ere I know what you will say to me.

BERNARD: Sit thee, please. My errand unto you is no delight, for I like thee well enough, 'tis true. So sit thee, please.

TIFFANIA: (*Looks around*) But where, my lord? Your chairs are charnel ground for the leavings of your business.

BERNARD: (*Realizes the two chairs are full of stuff*) Forgive my sloth. My servants, I fear, have fled south for the winter. (*Moves stuff off one chair onto the floor*) There. A throne it is not, but comfort for thy bottom it should give you.

TIFFANIA: Many thanks. My feet had grown weary. (*Looks around*) The wreckage of your working compels me to ask, might I busy myself in the ordering of your domain? If it please thee, I would be most swift in my ministrations upon the unruly host that haunteth you.

BERNARD: (*Sitting down heavily*) No, Tiffania. Such labor is not reserved for thee. You are a bright soul, your energy is like the sun at midday in August, but—

TIFFANIA: You are sending me out of the tower?

BERNARD: It grieveth me to say so, but I cannot deny the truth of your surmise.

TIFFANIA: Grieveth *you*? Why so, my lord? Your position is secure, your pockets heavy with gold. Of want you know nothing. On yon hill sits your mansion, and the good king has made solemn promise to you of an old age free of need. 'Tis I who should be quaking, for 'tis I who must venture forth into that bitter wind you named, with naught but these very rags.

BERNARD: Forgive me, Tiffania. My tongue fell into tired grooves. 'Twas a figure of speech, and yet it bore truth as well as custom.

TIFFANIA: O this is injustice cruel and cold. And now I've lost my chance to set the story true.

BERNARD: No, no. The book is not closed, the story as yet uncarved in stone. Prithee, paint the picture of your woe, and I will bend my ear to hear the truth.

Examples of Character Exercises

Examples

of

Character

Exercises

TIFFANIA: You will not judge me until all my words have lived in air?

BERNARD: I swear, Tiffania. *(Looks at his hourglass)* Speak the tale that e'en now dances on your eager lips.

TIFFANIA: But look here, you have more care for the slipping sand than for my desperate fate. How can I trust thee to hear me when your eyes are fixed on time?

BERNARD: *(Breaking)* List, my child. I might have sent a lesser man, a heartless hunter to cast you out without this chance to plead thy case. Do not harrass me with thy temper. The king's purse has spilled most precious silver to quench the thirst of your unseemly errors. Do not press my patience, nor overuse my love for thee. I have saved you from the dungeon. Be thankful and speak now quickly.

TIFFANIA: Forgive me, my lord. And many thanks for your kind intervention. 'Tis true the juggling of numbers was never my strength, though I labored valiantly to make it so. And when the cries came from the provinces for pennies to feed the hungry hordes, I sent queries unto you, and yet heard naught, and so the mother that lives in every woman's breast was sparked to life in me, and she did send forth the king's largesse. Can I be faulted for my nature that lives in my blood, that answers to the heart and not the head?

BERNARD: Which tallies with the summing of the exchequer. You are not cold-hearted enough to tend the shrunken pie of our nation's riches. You are meant to wed. To oversee a household. To raise children, and be a loving servant to your master.

TIFFANIA: And who, pray tell, might that master be? A man such as thee?

BERNARD: Oh, no, my child. I am old, my heart still wed to my departed muse. Yet my son, Rudolfo, he—

TIFFANIA: Forgive me, my lord. I would rather walk into the drifts of deepest snow, and pray with my last breath to be taken into heaven, than to countenance your son, who is to you a smear of ash next to the glorious cauldron of the sun.

BERNARD: Can these be truly your feelings, or is your tongue but the servant of fear?

TIFFANIA: Bring thy blessed bones to my chamber this eve, and we shall see whose fears take precedence. *[Exeunt]*

Interview to Create Character—*Partner Writing, page 110 (TW/MT)*

Tell us a little bit about your latest performance piece.
I'm in collaboration with a painter and a flute player. I start at the piano, she starts at her canvas, he stands center-stage with his flute, and we see what happens. We've taped five takes with the intent of editing some composite film, as well as preparing ourselves for a live tour. The last time we did it, I ended up hiding *in* the piano, the flute player was painting, and the painter was flat on his back.

What does it "mean"? Or is that not your concern?
It means whatever it means to whoever witnesses it. I certainly don't know what anything means, except to me. To my parents, it means I've lost my mind. When they paid my tuition to Juilliard year after year, this is not what they felt they were preparing me for.

Does that bother you, what they or anyone else thinks of your work? Are you free of that sort of self-editing, based on others' views or criticisms?
No. I'm what my friend calls an adulation slut. Despite my apparent abandonment of "normal" process, I still desperately crave approval and acceptance. That's the irony in most artists' work. Intellectually, we know that mass approval is almost a sure sign we're not cutting-edge, but mass disapproval is no indicator of avante greatness. It may just mean we're making garbage. It's all a great psychological muddle.

Do you read much psychology?
I've read Jung through and through. And I've been reading a bit

of Buddhist psychology, which completely erases the boundary we've created in the West between mind and spirit. In that sense, Jung was something of a Buddhist, I suppose.

Are you a Buddhist, an anarchist, or a revolutionary?
You know, I'm what I call a soft human. I believe in tenderness and generosity. I guess that makes me a bit of all those things. I want to heal, not to hurt.

Experimenting with Narrative Boundaries—*Basic Exercise, page 112 (TW)*

2. List of traits and narrative boundaries.

   - American

   - Knows the life histories of all his characters

   - Knows what his main character is thinking and feeling

   - Other characters reveal their thoughts and feelings through dialogue and action

   - Nonjudgmental

   - Minimally descriptive

3. Draft a third-person story in the voice of this narrator.

   Will had come to Land's End to be by himself. To his chagrin, he found a sailboat race taking place just off the point where he'd hoped to sit and write a letter to Mary, his wife of twenty years. The low cliffs and rocky beach were crowded with noisy people—the parents and siblings of the junior sailors in their small, white crafts.

   "Dammit," he said, feeling cheated. He'd come three hundred miles to be alone and out of range of Mary's psychic presence. He intended to leave her as soon as he'd stated his case to her in writing. He loved her, though he loathed being married to her. She suffered from chronic fatigue and manic depression. *She is more symptom than woman,* he often thought to himself.

   A woman shrieked, shattering Will's unhappy reverie. He looked out at the pod of little boats and saw that one had capsized. Its sailor, a girl, had clambered up out of the water onto the side of her boat, its hull made of some floatable synthetic. A motor launch was making its slow way through the sailboats to rescue her.

"Too windy for racing," said someone at Will's elbow, the voice elderly and gruff, impossible to classify by gender. "I told them so. She won't be the last to go down."

"Seems a long way from anywhere to have a race," said Will, scowling at the little boats before turning to see who he was speaking to. "Why here?"

"Weekenders," said the old woman, her shock of stiff white hair resisting the offshore breeze. "They know nothing about the sea."

"Do you live around here?" asked Will, hoping the woman might direct him to a more secluded spot.

"I've lived nowhere else," said the old woman, squinting out at the shining waters. "I went to London once. Madness. Sheer madness."

"Yes," said Will, nodding wearily. "I've lived there for thirty years."

"If you can call it living," said the old woman, closing one eye as she turned to look at him. "Looking for solitude are you?"

"Yes," he said, nodding eagerly. "Do you know a place nearby? I'm sick of driving."

"My place," she said, nodding slowly. "I'm the lighthouse keeper. Not a soul out my way but me and my child."

4. Modified list of traits and narrative boundaries.

- British

- Long sentences

- Expansively descriptive

- Allows characters to reveal themselves primarily through actions and dialogue

5. Rewritten story in voice of modified narrator.

Will Abrams, a tall, slender man with longish gray hair, a deeply furrowed brow, close-set brown eyes, and a long, slender nose, stood on the edge of a crumbling sandstone cliff some fifty feet above a rocky beach, his unhappy gaze fixed on a pod of little sailboats racing in a stiff wind, each craft sporting a crew of one—a teenaged boy or girl.

On the beach, amidst the gray boulders and wild tangles of driftwood and seaweed, and all along the cliff for hundreds of yards in either direction, families had gathered in support of the young sailors. There were portable barbecues filling the air with the smells of hot dogs and hamburgers, and white smoke tinged with the scent of lighter fluid. From the shining sea came the voice of the race supervisor, calling out instructions and warnings to the racers in his stentorian baritone.

Will had come to this heretofore remote spot—Land's End—to rid himself of people, and so this great crowd was an affront to his desires. He cursed in a loud whisper, and just as he did so, one of the boats capsized, spilling a girl into the roiling sea, which caused a woman not ten feet from Will to shriek in dismay and leap to her feet, crying, "Angela! Oh my Angela."

To everyone's immediate relief, the soggy mariner, a long-armed girl of vigorous dexterity, clambered up onto the side of her unsinkable craft and calmly awaited the arrival of a rumbling motor launch deployed expressly for such rescue missions.

"Seems a long way from anywhere to have a race," said Will, scowling at the boats without really seeing them. He wished, through his dissatisfaction, to banish them into thin air. He was so very tired of nothing turning out the way he hoped it would. "Why here?"

"Weekenders," said an elderly woman at Will's elbow, her voice gruff and masculine, her heavy brown coat several sizes too large for her tiny frame. "They know nothing of the sea."

"Do you live around here?" asked Will, hoping the odd old woman might know of a more secluded spot.

"All my life," said the woman, scanning the shining waters with her deeply knowing eyes. "I went to London once. For three days. It was madness. Sheer madness."

"Yes," said Will, his voice betraying his weariness, his mind clogged with visions of Mary and their dark, old house. "I've lived there for thirty years."

"If you can call it living," said the old woman, closing one eye and biting her lower lip. "Looking for quiet, aren't you?"

"Yes," he said, feeling pleasantly lulled by her voice. "Do you know a place nearby? I dread more driving."

"My place," she said, turning away from the sea in such a way that he could not help but follow her.

"Oh, but I wouldn't want to impose on—"

"I'm the lighthouse keeper," she said, ignoring his tired politeness. "Cassie's Cove. The beach there is sheltered from the wind. Not a soul for miles around, save for me and my child. And we won't bother. Come on."

Examples

of

Character

Exercises

Honoring the Roughness of Your Rough Drafts

I may change everything I write about honoring your rough draft.

Every word of this little essay may end up changed in the final form of the essay and the redundancy of using the word *essay* may be taken care of in the second or third or eleventh draft, but for now I don't have to worry about that because this is a rough draft.

Anything goes in a rough draft or it isn't a rough draft.

Imagine wearing your finest clothes and being very careful not to get dirty after you've decided to go play in the mud. That's connected somehow to this rough draft. Try that again.

So, you've decided to go play in the mud. Do you put on your fanciest clothes, your most precious, fragile jewelry, and approach the mud puddle with the hope of not getting dirty?

Rough drafts might be called "freedom from judgment" drafts. Rough drafts are invitations to try anything.

I love the rough-draft phase of story writing because out of my freewriting may come all sorts of unexpected ideas or words or directions. I've written ten pages of prose from which a good four-line poem emerged. If I'd set out to write that four-line poem I might never have gotten it. Poems turn into stories, exercises turn into essays, all sorts of creations manifest when we give ourselves permission to write whatever wants to be written.

When the judge or the critic or the part of my brain that worries about what other people are going to think about my writing intrudes on my rough draft, I say, "Ah, there you are again. Go away. I may call on my editor at some later date, but for now I'm writing free."

Honor the roughness of your rough draft. Out of that roughness you may carve and polish and extract and rewrite. Out of that roughness you may cut the gems. But for now let the roughness be as rough as it will be.

Enough said.⤳TW

$\mathcal{S}$TORY

*The universe is made of
stories, not of atoms.*
—MURIEL RUKEYSER

Wouldn't it be wonderful if stories flowed effortlessly from our pens? Impossible? Not at all. The exercises described in this chapter will help you tap into the virtually limitless supply of stories in the treasure trove of your imagination.

TELLING STORIES

We are all storytellers. We are constantly telling each other about our lives—what happened to us, what we saw, what we thought. We share news of dramatic events in our lives and in the lives of our friends. We tell jokes. We share dreams and memories. Starting with these kinds of "tellings" can be a good way to begin our practice of writing stories.

What Just Happened to You?

1. Take a few minutes to say aloud something that happened to you in the hour before you sat down to write—something you did, something you witnessed, somewhere you went.

Basic Exercise
(example on page 170)

Try doing this exercise as a letter to your best friend.

2. As you speak, jot down occasional words or phrases from your telling that seem significant.

3. Now *write* what happened to you. Try to write conversationally, as if you were speaking. Refer to the words or phrases you jotted down to help you write your story.

4. Read your story aloud. Make changes or add details—fictional or actual—that make the story more to your liking.

VARIATION 1. For a longer exercise, make each of your sentences into the first sentence of a paragraph. Complete these paragraphs.

VARIATION 2. After reading your story aloud, change some of the details and write a new story.

For Partners: Tell each other what just happened to you. Act as secretaries for each other, jotting down key phrases and details of the tellings. Give each other these notes and use them to help you write your stories.

For Groups: Have one person in the group tell about what just happened to her. When she's done, each of you write a version of her story, adding details and plot twists of your own. Take turns reading your stories aloud.

Jokes

Most good jokes are very short stories that happen to be funny. They have a beginning, a middle, a climax, and an end. They almost always involve a cast of characters and an intriguing situation. And most importantly, their success is largely dependent on how well they are told.

Basic Exercise (example on page 172)

1. Tell a joke out loud.

2. Think about the joke and spontaneously give it a title.

3. Now write the joke down as if you are transcribing your telling of it.

4. Read the joke aloud and make any changes you feel are necessary to make it sound better.

VARIATION 1. Write what happens to the main character *after* the joke (story) ends.

VARIATION 2. Rewrite the joke, setting it in another time and place.

VARIATION 3. Use the plot of the joke to write a similar story that ends differently and isn't necessarily funny.

Dreams

Dreams are stories, or parts of stories, that come to us in our sleep. One of the great things about dream imagery is that it springs from the subconscious—a source much less inhibited than the conscious mind. The things we see and do in our dreams, however "weird" or "crazy," can lead to wonderful stories or story forms.

Note: There are numerous techniques to help you improve your dream recall. See "Dream On" on page 147.

1. Using first person, present tense, tell your dream out loud; for example:

   I am lost in a huge building. Strange noises are coming from...

2. Give your dream a title.

3. Write down the dream, using first person, present tense.

4. Divide your dream into three parts, calling them Beginning, Middle, and End. Still using first person, present tense, create details to expand each section.

Basic Exercise

(example on page 174)

VARIATION 1. Complete the first three steps. After reading your dream aloud, invent what happens next.

VARIATION 2. Complete the exercise. For an additional step, rewrite your expanded dream story in third person, past tense; for example:

   Harold, a tall slender man with frightened eyes, was lost in an enormous old castle. He could hear the squeaking of a thousand bats coming from behind...

VARIATION 3: Use the form of your dream to create an Arbitrary Story Structure (see page 148).

For Partners: Tell each other a memorable dream. Act as secretaries for each other, jotting down key phrases and details of the dreams. Each of you write a short story combining some of the details from your two dreams.

For Groups: Have one member tell a dream. Using Circle Writing (page 28), co-create stories beginning with the last image of the dream.

EARLIEST MEMORIES

There are numerous exercises throughout this book that tap the rich resources of our memories. "Our Bliss" (page 103) and "Our Fears" (page 106) focus on specific *kinds* of memories. Here we will use the earliest memories we can access.

Basic Exercise
(examples on pages 177–178)

1. Take a few moments to relax. Affirm your wish to remember as far back in time as you can.

2. Quickly, without censoring yourself, make a list of the first seven things or events that come to mind—a few words for each item. As you make this list, you may find yourself opening to all sorts of memories. If a memory from the recent past comes up, write that down, too.

3. Read this list to yourself, then spontaneously choose one of the seven items to focus on.

4. Take a minute or so to write some of the details you remember surrounding this memory. These details may be single words, sentence fragments, bits of dialogue, anything that comes to mind.

5. Using these details, write a narrative account of this memory, using first person, present tense; for example:

   I am four years old, standing at the kitchen door. I am looking out at a growling dog: a big, brown hound with bloodshot eyes.

Almost all writers, at one time or another, are struck wordless by the specter of the blank page. Where will we find the next story or poem or essay idea? What could we possibly write that's interesting and new? Fortunately, there is a source of original ideas that's available to all of us, all the time: our dreams.

Dreams are a wonderful form of storytelling—infinitely inventive, rich in detail, fresh and uncensored. In our dreams we connect with the vast mystery of Being and can discover truths about ourselves and others, about Life in all its terror and beauty, that might otherwise escape our notice.

Many people say they don't dream, but the truth is they just don't remember. Science has proven that every one of us dreams every night of our lives. If you don't have automatic dream recall, the simple decision to pay more attention will make your dreams more available to you. Begin to think of the recollection of dreams as part of your research as a writer, and the door to your dreams will open.

There are simple techniques for tapping this limitless inner lode. Begin by placing a notebook by your bedside. Before falling asleep each night, repeat several times to yourself that you intend to remember your dreams upon awakening. If you wake up in the middle of the night with dream images in your mind, take a moment to jot them down before going back to sleep. Key words and phrases will be enough to help you reconstruct the dream later on.

In the morning, while still in bed, make it your first order of business to record a dream (or two or three), even if you remember it only vaguely. Write in first person, present tense to capture the immediacy of the dream experience. (For example, "I am running down a long purple-sand beach crowded with seagulls as big as cows.") Include as much detail as you can: colors, textures, shapes, and sounds—every little thread is important in the tapestry of a dream. Don't stop to edit or analyze, just write down the experience as if it were currently happening to you.

You may remember only a few details at first, but as you continue writing you will recollect more and more pieces of the dream story. After you've recorded all you can remember, read the dream story aloud and instinctively write down a title for it. Don't think about what the title should be, just quickly write a word or phrase that comes to mind.

In most dreams there is at least one detail that will capture your curiosity—perhaps a cryptic comment made by one of the dream's characters (record it word-for-word, if possible) or a bizarre image, like a tree with pencils dangling like fruit from its branches. Make special note of these oddities. Also note the emotional tone at specific points during the dream: Did you feel calm while being chased by snarling coyotes? Were you angry while rushing a flaming pumpkin between towering blue goalposts? These emotions are clues to the dream's deeper meanings.

For some, dream work is so rewarding it becomes an important part of life. If this is true for you, there are many books that can guide you in deepening the process. But even if you record and study your dreams only occasionally, the practice will inspire and energize your writing.ॐMT

(For writing exercises using dream material, see "Dreams," page 145.)

Dream

On

Variation 1. Fill your initial list with **names** of people you remember, including some telling detail about each of them.

1. Bernie—loved hot mustard
2. Bernice—funny faces

Choose one of these people, and repeat the exercise using them as your focus.

Variation 2. Choose three items from your list and write a story combining these three items.

Variation 3. When you are satisfied with your narrative, make it the middle of a story. Now write the beginning and the end.

For Partners: Write a three-line Exchange Story (see "Partner Writing," page 25) in which each of you begins a story with three lines of a real memory. Exchange pages, and continue the narratives with three lines *not* from your memories, but imagined. Continue exchanging pages, mixing the real with the imagined until you both feel your pieces are complete.

For Groups: Do the basic exercise as solo writers, then read your creations aloud. After everyone has finished reading, do ten minutes of free-writing (see "Free-writing," page xiv).

Arbitrary Story Structures

To help writers overcome one of the most fundamental obstacles to successful story writing, we devised a simple and effective story-generating technique that frees the writer from having to invent the structure of a story before she begins to write it. When a writer is relieved of the need to invent a plot, her intuitive talents are free to emerge.

Arbitrary Story Structures are *not* detailed plots, but rather bare skeletons on which to hang an original tale. Following the brief instructions, we present eight structures of varying complexity. Each of them is written in a particular person and tense, but feel free to use any tense or person you prefer. Some of the structures provide slightly more specific suggestions than others. Use the ones you find most appealing.

B a s i c
E x e r c i s e
(example on page 179)

1. Read Part 1 of the Arbitrary Story Structure and write the first paragraph of your story.

2. Read Part 2 and write the second paragraph of your story.

3. Continue this process until you've written a paragraph for each part of the structure.

4. Read your story aloud.

5. If you like some or all of your story, refine or expand it.

Arbitrary Story Structure 1: The Journey

Part 1. You are on your way somewhere.

Part 2. You see something that strikes you as extraordinary.

Part 3. You think about what you've seen.

Part 4. You encounter another person.

Part 5. You have a brief conversation with this person.

Part 6. You fall asleep and dream. Tell the dream.

Arbitrary Story Structure 2: The Turning Point

Part 1. Someone is somewhere.

Part 2. He thinks about something and decides to go somewhere.

Part 3. He reaches the destination.

Part 4. He experiences a strong emotion.

Part 5. He has a vivid memory.

Part 6. He does something uncharacteristic.

Arbitrary Story Structure 3: Eavesdropping

Part 1. You are on your way somewhere.

Part 2. You overhear a conversation.

Part 3. You think about what you've overheard.

Part 4. You change course.

Arbitrary Story Structure 4: Pieces of Dreams

Part 1. You remembered the very end of a dream.

Part 2. You looked in the mirror and had a long thought.

Part 3. You made a phone call.

Part 4. You set out on a journey.

Part 5. You remembered more of your dream.

Arbitrary Story Structure 5: Remembering

Part 1. Someone was somewhere.

Part 2. She ate something and thought about her past.

Part 3. She got dressed and recalled something someone once told her.

Part 4. Then she was somewhere else.

Part 5. She watched someone and imagined some things about the person's life.

Part 6. She realized something about herself.

Arbitrary Story Structure 6: Past and Present Merge

Part 1. You are sitting somewhere, having a favorite drink.

Part 2. You remember something your mother said to you and the circumstances surrounding her saying it.

Part 3. Someone approaches and speaks to you.

Part 4. You answer and a conversation ensues.

Part 5. You are walking somewhere, thinking about the person you had the conversation with.

Part 6. You remember something about the conversation.

Part 7. You find something in your path that answers a question.

Arbitrary Story Structure 7: The Gift

Part 1. A person is angry about something.

Part 2. A child says something to the angry person.

Part 3. Whatever the person was angry about takes on a new meaning.

Part 4. The person sees his reflection and tells himself something.

Arbitrary Story Structure 8: The Riddle

Part 1. You were confused about something.

Part 2. Someone took your picture.

Part 3. You remembered lines from a song.

Part 4. You decided to contact someone you hadn't spoken to in a long time.

Part 5. An elderly person said something to you.

Part 6. You wanted to remember something, but couldn't.

Part 7. You heard a sound that brought back the memory.

Part 8. Whatever you were confused about became clearer.

Part 9. You remembered a riddle.

For Partners and Groups: Arbitrary Story Structures work wonderfully for both Partner Writing (page 25) and Circle Writing (page 28). (Also see "Inventing Your Own Structures," page 154.)

ABSTRACT STORY STRUCTURES

Each step of an *Abstract* Story Structure consists of a single evocative word, rather than a specific action as in the *Arbitrary* Story Structures (page 148). Some writers immediately take to abstract structures, while others benefit from practicing first with arbitrary structures.

Basic Exercise	

1. Read the first part of the structure. Allow a moment for the word to bring an image or thought to mind. Now write the first paragraph of your story.

2. Repeat this process for each of the parts of the structure.

3. Read your story aloud.

4. If you like some or all of your story, refine or expand it.

Abstract Story Structure 1

Part 1. Child
Part 2. Sister
Part 3. Man
Part 4. Garden
Part 5. Memory

Abstract Story Structure 2

Part 1. Morning
Part 2. Rain
Part 3. Journey
Part 4. Obstacle
Part 5. Mother
Part 6. Accident
Part 7. Harvest

Abstract Story Structure 3

Part 1. Home
Part 2. Ghost
Part 3. Door
Part 4. View
Part 5. Friend
Part 6. Desire
Part 7. Conversation
Part 8. Happiness
Part 9. Path

Abstract Story Structure 4

Part 1. Fruit
Part 2. Restaurant
Part 3. Alley
Part 4. Song
Part 5. Father
Part 6. Water
Part 7. Rock
Part 8. Souvenir
Part 9. Surprise
Part 10. Cat

Abstract Story Structure 5

Part 1. Laughter
Part 2. Forgetting
Part 3. Anger
Part 4. Rolling
Part 5. Lost
Part 6. Hill
Part 7. Changing
Part 8. Beginning

Abstract Story Structure 6

Part 1. Injury
Part 2. Visitor
Part 3. Messages
Part 4. Anecdote
Part 5. Brother
Part 6. Animal
Part 7. Glimpse
Part 8. Love

INVENTING YOUR OWN STRUCTURES

Once we become comfortable with allowing single words or suggested actions to inspire our stories, a natural next step is the creation of our own structures.

The purpose of a structure is to provide an initial direction for your narrative. However, if the story takes on a momentum of its own and moves away from your arbitrary or abstract structure, by all means follow the new direction and see where it goes. You can always come back to, or modify, your structure should you find your momentum slowing or stopping.

Though most of the structures presented in the sections on Arbitrary and Abstract Story Structures were tested and refined over time, a few of them were invented spontaneously, by simply listing possible parts for a story as they occurred to us. We call these spontaneous inventions "Random Structures."

Note: The following exercises will be easier to understand if you first read "Arbitrary Story Structures" (page 148) and "Abstract Story Structures" (page 152).

Random Structures

<table>
<tr>
<td>

*Basic
Exercise*
(example on page 183)

</td>
<td>

1. On a blank sheet of paper, write "Part 1." Without taking more than a moment to think, write down a single evocative word or a phrase suggesting some action to inspire the first part of a story. For instance:

</td>
</tr>
</table>

Someone is on a train
or
I wake up depressed
or
clock

2. Below Part 1, write "Part 2," then write down the next arbitrary or abstract part that occurs to you. This part need not have a logical connection to the previous part, though it might. For instance:

Someone gets dressed
or
I decide to change careers
or
daybreak

3. Below Part 2, write "Part 3," then write down the next arbitrary or abstract part that occurs to you.

4. Continue this process until you have a seven-part structure.

5. Use your random structure to write the first draft of a story.

For Partners: Create a Random Structure by taking turns suggesting parts. When you have at least five parts, each of you write a story following the structure. You may also use this structure for Partner Writing (see page 25).

For Groups: Create a Random Structure by going around the circle, asking each member to suggest one part in the structure. Have everyone in the group write a story using the same structure. You may also utilize this structure for Circle Writing (see page 28).

Creating Your Structure as You Go

1. Quickly and spontaneously write down an arbitrary or abstract part in a story. For instance:

Basic Exercise

> *When you find yourself struggling with a sentence or a paragraph— when something about the order or rhythm of the words doesn't seem quite right—try reading out loud what you've written.*

Someone hears a strange sound
or
I am struggling to remember a woman's name
or
California

2. Using this arbitrary or abstract part to prompt you, write the first paragraph or two of your story.

3. Read what you've written.

4. Now write another arbitrary or abstract part that springs from what you've written so far.

5. Prompted by this second part, write the second paragraph of your story.

6. Repeat this process—inventing parts as you go—until you feel satisfied with what you've written.

7. If you like some or all of your story, refine or expand it.

For Partners: Begin this exercise with one of you calling out an arbitrary or abstract part. Now both of you begin a story based on that part. When you've both completed a first paragraph, the other partner calls out the next part, and so on. You may also wish to use this technique for Partner Writing (page 25).

For Groups: Begin by having one member call out an arbitrary or abstract part. When everyone in the group has completed the first paragraph of a story prompted by this first part, have another member call out the next part, and so on. You may also use this technique for Circle Writing (page 28).

NATURAL STORY STRUCTURES

The human life cycle—birth, life, death—is a grand story structure to which many of the world's most famous novels adhere. Within this most familiar structure, countless story lines wait to support your unique visions. And beyond the human life cycle, in the patterns of all things, myriad story structures await you.

What, for instance, is the abstract structure of a day? Here is a seven-part abstract structure based on one of many possible interpretations.

Part 1. Darkness

Part 2. Dawn

Part 3. Morning

Part 4. Noon

Part 5. Afternoon

Part 6. Evening

Part 7. Night

To make a less abstract structure, we might expand the parts thusly:

Part 1. Someone is lying awake in the middle of the night.

Part 2. At dawn, they make an important decision.

Part 3. On their way to work, they witness an accident.

Part 4. About to leave for lunch, they have a fight with their boss.

Part 5. Suddenly fired, they spend the afternoon at the zoo.

Part 6. They go see a movie with a new friend and disagree violently about it.

Part 7. As they prepare for bed, they get a phone call from an old friend.

Though the story that springs from this structure may not be *about* a day, it will be imbued with the deeply familiar, organic form *of* a day, which will make it resonate—at least subliminally—with both writer and reader.

Place and Practice

On a train traveling west, stopped at a nowhere station waiting for repairs, I am glad for the thousandth time that I always carry a notebook in my bag. I lay it on my lap, uncap my pen, lean back, and rest my eyes for a moment on the yellowing late-summer fields outside my window. Finding myself captive in a thoroughly comfortable situation has a calming effect on my mind and body. I get a bit sleepy but remain alert. There is no escape, so I may as well relax. Nothing to do but wait for whatever comes next. To wait and to write. The words that flow onto the page during this suspended hour are languid and dreamy.

Another time, choosing a bench near an ancient stone wall in a churchyard, I sit gazing at a luxurious garden, vibrant gladioli and roses dipping and swaying in the strong breeze. Here, nature themes dominate my journal pages. I record some early flower memories, sketch a maple tree, and lose myself in the drafting of a butterfly poem—its language lavish and sensual.

Now, on the same bench but with my back to the garden, I let the old wall still my mind with its utter tranquillity. After half an hour of meditation, I produce a few haiku—short poems stripped of every extraneous sound and image. Quite unlike the garden, the wall stimulates concise, unadorned expression.

As these personal recollections illustrate, place can have a profound impact on our writing. We are impressionable creatures, and when we open ourselves to the particular sights and sounds, colors and textures of our surroundings, a sense of the place can be discerned in the writing we do there.

"Found" places often provoke interesting writing, arousing unusual emotions and ideas. Here's an exercise that may help when you feel blocked in your writing. Set out walking with a notebook and pen until you find a place that entices you: perhaps a bench near a bustling playground or a grassy tuft beneath an old oak tree in the county park. Sit quietly for a few minutes, taking in the landscape, the people or other creatures, the energy of the place—then let the writing flow out, whatever it may be. Allow this out-of-the-ordinary location to draw from you whatever words it will.

For ongoing practice, many people find is useful to establish a regular writing place. For them, consistency of place encourages consistency of practice. Over time, your routine writing spot may come to possess an almost mystical capacity to get you going.

Some writers insist on the controlled atmosphere of a private space for their regular practice, be it an opulent studio, a cramped bedroom corner, or a hammock in the backyard. These people do their best writing in that one spot and nowhere else. Others find their perfect writing places out in the world; the boisterous mood of a busy cafe, for example, triggers in some writers a state of intense concentration on the page in progress. They lay claim to a certain table every other morning at ten and know the espresso-master by name.

What works best for you? The only way to find out is to experiment with different settings and notice what the various places inspire you to express. Eventually, you'll discover the locations most conducive to your writing practice. ⋙MT

1. Choose one of the phenomena listed below and create an Abstract Structure by breaking it down into your notion of its parts.

   * Preparing a meal

   * A love affair

   * Going fishing

   * Pregnancy

   * A day at school

   * A sunset

   * A river

   * An argument

   * A honeybee's life

   * The life cycle of a plant

2. If you feel inspired by this Abstract Structure, attempt a story from it, following the instructions for Abstract Story Structures, page 152.

3. If you wish to create a less abstract structure, expand each of your abstract parts into a more detailed part for an Arbitrary Story Structure (see page 148).

4. Write a story using the structure you've created.

DIAGRAMMING THE STRUCTURES OF FAVORITE BOOKS AND STORIES

Some writers have expressed concern that diagramming the structure of a favorite story or book and then writing something based on the structure might be a form of plagiarism. We have no such misgivings because each writer who undertakes this process will create a completely original variation.

Basic Exercise

(example on page 184)

1. Read a story you love, then go back through it and create an Abstract Structure by writing a list of single words that capture the progression of the story.

2. Expand this Abstract Story Structure into an Arbitrary Story Structure by expanding the words into phrases that suggest actions.

3. Write a new story, from either your Abstract or your Arbitrary Story Structure.

For Partners: Each of you diagram the same story, then write your stories from each other's diagrams.

STORIES FROM VISUALS

The first books we see as children are picture books with little or no text. We then progress to books containing more words and fewer pictures. Finally, we begin to read books with no pictures. Along the way, we are learning to "see" the story while reading the words. Conversely, looking at pictures and photographs will often bring stories to mind—stories we might want to write down.

Stories from a Single Image

The world abounds in images. Newspapers contain photographs. Magazines and billboards feature a vast array of dazzling imagery. Your family photo album preserves pictures of you and your past. Bookstores and libraries contain many volumes of images. Museums and galleries house splendid works of art. Using intriguing images to create a story can be a rich and satisfying process.

Basic Exercise

(examples on pages 192–193)

1. Find an image that stirs you—a person, a thing, a place, a crowd scene, an incident, anything you like.

2. Study the image carefully. Let your eyes travel slowly over every part of it, taking in all the details.

3. Keeping the image in mind, close your eyes and imagine what was happening just *before* the action depicted in the image occurred.

4. Look at the image again.

5. Close your eyes and imagine what might have happened *after* the action depicted in the image occurred.

6. Spontaneously write a story that springs from the image.

VARIATION 1. If there is a person in the image, try writing the story in his or her voice.

VARIATION 2. Create an Arbitrary Story Structure inspired by the image, and use that structure to write your story. (See "Inventing Your Own Structures," page 154.)

VARIATION 3. Create a story in which the image depicts the first scene of your story.

VARIATION 4. Create a story in which the image depicts the final scene of your story.

For Partners: Find a picture you think would be fun or challenging for your partner to base a story on. With both of you referring to the same image, write an Exchange Story. (See "Partner Writing," page 25.)

For Groups: Have everyone bring images they find compelling. Select one of the images, and have everyone write a story from the same image. Share your stories. You might also do a Circle Writing process, referring to the image. (See "Circle Writing," page 28.)

Stories from a Series of Images

This exercise is another way of creating an Arbitrary Story Structure (page 148). By gathering several images, you will have the inspiration for several parts of a story. These images need not be related to each other in any obvious way, though it's fine if they are.

1. Find five images that stir you. These might be photographs, paintings, postcards—any visual representations. You

Basic Exercise

might choose a photo, a drawing, a postcard, and an illustration from a book, or you might choose five photographs. Any combination of images is fine.

2. Take a few moments to put the images into some kind of order. You can do this randomly or intuitively. Try not to take too long with this part of the process.

3. When you have your images arranged, begin a story by looking at the first image and writing a paragraph.

4. Look at the second image, then write the second paragraph. Allow the images to guide your imagination.

5. Continue this process until you have written a paragraph for each of the images.

6. Read your story aloud.

7. If you like your story, refine or expand it.

VARIATION 1. Reverse the order of your images, and write a new story.

VARIATION 2. Keep the first image the same, but mix up the order of the other images, and write a new story.

VARIATION 3. Try this exercise with ten images.

For Partners: Each of you bring three images to your meeting. Combine the six images in some kind of order from which you both write a story, or from which you cocreate stories using Partner Writing (page 25).

For Groups: This is a good exercise to do on the same night you do the Postcard exercises (page 49). Each person contributes a postcard to the sequence of images, then everyone writes a story from the same sequence.

Stories from Drawings You Make

Inexplicable alchemy can take place when we combine drawing with writing. Even if you don't do much (or any) drawing, please give this exercise a try. You might be surprised by what you write as a result of exercising your drawing muscles. Don't worry about your drawings being "good." It is the *act* of drawing that catalyzes the story-writing flow.

1. On a blank piece of paper, without using a model, quickly draw a person's face. This will be a character in the story you are about to write.

2. Below the face, write a name that seems to fit the face.

3. Below the character's name, quickly draw a picture of something else—anything. This might be another view of the same person, another person, an object, a place.

4. Below this second drawing, write a word or two describing what it is.

5. Referring to these two drawings, write a story that involves the person and the other thing you drew.

6. Read aloud.

VARIATION 1. Looking at the two drawings, create an Arbitrary Story Structure (page 148) from which to write a story.

VARIATION 2. Make three quick sketches of faces. Choose your favorite face and write a story in the voice of this character.

VARIATION 3. Make five quick sketches of people or things. Next to each image write whatever it calls to your mind—these might be words, phrases, or story fragments. Use some or all of these elements to create a story or a story structure.

For Partners: Each of you begin a drawing on a blank page. Exchange pages. Add something to each other's drawings. Exchange pages five times. Use these two co-created drawings to do VARIATION 1 above. You may also wish to use these drawings to do the exercise described under Stories from a Single Image (page 160).

For Groups: Take fifteen minutes to doodle and draw, making several sketches of people and things. Each of you choose one of your drawings as your contribution to a sequence of images for doing the Stories from a Series of Images exercise (page 161).

BEGINNINGS

Many writers struggle to begin a story because they want to get their first sentence "just right" before they create the rest of their opus. This is an understandable desire, but it can be a major impediment to writing a story. When we realize that all of our writing is meaningful practice, the first sentence is merely a way to begin, not the most important of all sentences.

Besides, by the time we've completed the first draft, our story concept will have evolved, and we may decide to abandon our original beginning altogether.

The First Sentence

Basic Exercise
(examples on pages 194–195)

1. Quickly write a first sentence.

2. Read the sentence and see what story begins to arise from this opening line. Now write the rest of the first paragraph of your story.

3. Read your paragraph. Now underline a sentence (or sentence fragment) in the paragraph that seems most essential to the story.

4. Make this sentence or fragment the new opening of your story. Write a new first paragraph that springs from this new opening, telling the same story differently.

5. Read your new paragraph. Choose the single *word* that seems most essential to the story you are telling.

6. Now write a new first sentence containing your chosen word, then write a new paragraph inspired by this sentence, telling the same story differently.

VARIATION 1. Repeat steps 1 and 2. Skip step 3, and for a new step 4, use the *last* sentence of the initial paragraph for your new first sentence. Repeat steps 5 and 6.

VARIATION 2. Repeat the basic exercise, allowing yourself to begin an *entirely different* story with each new opening line.

The First Page

1. Write the first page of a story. You may use an Arbitrary Story Structure (page 148) to create this first page.

2. Read what you've written. Put this first page away and write another first page, beginning the same story again. Start the story in much the same way as you did before, or try a new approach.

3. Read what you've written. Put this second first page away and write another first page, beginning the same story once more. Again, begin your story as you did before, or try a new approach.

Basic Exercise

(example on page 196)

Endings

"I'm having trouble with my ending."

"What's the trouble?"

"Well, I think it needs more punch."

"Does the rest of your story have enough punch for you?"

"I think it will with a strong ending."

"What is a strong ending?"

"Something surprising and dramatic."

"Is the rest of your story surprising and dramatic?"

"It could be with a powerful ending."

"Where would the power of the ending come from if not from the rest of your story? If a reader doesn't care about your characters by the middle of the story, why would she suddenly care at the end?"

"So it's about the characters?"

"Perhaps, but...Here's what I believe: The very best way to write a strong ending is to write a strong beginning, and then sustain the tone and pace and essence of that beginning until the story or poem feels complete."

⸎TW

4. Read all three of your first pages aloud. What elements remained the same? What changed? Imagine how the three finished stories would differ.

Variation 1. Choose one of your three beginnings and continue writing the story from that point.

Variation 2. Craft a new first page, using your favorite parts from each of your drafts, then continue writing the story from that point.

Variation 3. Choose one of your three beginnings. Write a new paragraph to *precede* your beginning.

Interview to Create a Story

An interview is a wonderful way to generate the plot and various other details of a story. (Our Basic Interview Process is described on page 32. An example of an interview used to create a story can be found on page 198.)

Here are twenty questions, some of which you might find useful for eliciting a story from yourself or your writing partner.

1. Who are you?

2. What are you?

3. What happened to you?

4. Why do you think it happened?

5. What was the day like?

6. What was going on in the rest of the world?

7. What was your mood?

8. Where exactly did this happen?

9. Who else was involved?

10. Was it a surprise?

11. Was it illegal?

12. Were you frightened?

13. How long did it last?

14. Was it your idea?

15. Then what happened?

16. How did you feel while it was happening?

17. When did you know it was over?

18. What would you do differently next time?

19. What did you learn from all this?

20. What do you think might happen now?

If you're interested in writing a play, and you've written some short stories you like, consider translating your stories into play form. Most contemporary two-act plays are structurally akin to short stories, with a handful of characters and actions taking place in the course of a day or two, rather than over months or years, as is the case with many novels.

By the same token, if you're struggling with rewriting or finishing a play, try writing your play as a story and honing it in that form to help you overcome any structural difficulties. ᠊ᠵᠥTW

A

Dramatic

Trick

ARBITRARY OR ABSTRACT NOVEL STRUCTURES

This exercise will give you some experience of the complexity of the novel-writing process. Before beginning, read our sections on Arbitrary Story Structures (page 148) and Abstract Story Structures (page 152).

1. Create a thirty-step arbitrary or abstract story structure, thinking of each step as the central idea for a chapter.

The Poetic Outline

Many of us associate outlining with the drudgery of schoolwork, but the outline can be a fluid, poetic, incredibly helpful tool for creating a structure for your novella, novel, play, or screenplay.

Here is a brief description of my poetic outlining process:

I am sitting on a park bench overlooking San Francisco Bay. A strong breeze is blowing in through the Golden Gate. I've finally cleared the boards to begin work on a new novel that has been forming itself in my mind for several weeks. In a small notebook, with a fine-tipped black pen, I write the title *The Taker* at the top of the page. This title came to me in a dream and was confirmed during my meditations this morning.

Below the title I write

1. *he meets her, a flurry of images, nothing certain*

2. *in her garden, he speaks of birds, she speaks of death*

3. *away from her, the weight of his past takes hold, wanting to see her again*

This process—without judgment, without editing—flows on and on. As I write I begin to see my characters, hear their voices, discover nuances of their thoughts and actions, feel the energy of their feelings. I give myself to this jotting, knowing it is the roughest of rough drafts, knowing it is an invitation to the spirits to tell their story through me.

When the flow stops, I read my outline and jot down other details that come to mind.

1. he meets her, a flurry of images, nothing certain,
   shy, graceful man, calico cat, long skirt, a scar on her cheek

2. in her garden, he speaks of birds, she speaks of death,
   sun after rain, cottage entangled in blackberries, father

3. away from her, the weight of his past takes hold, wanting to see her again,
   thinking of her —a jolt of recognition—he finds the will to move on

If I'm in love with what has come out of this process, I will begin to write the novel. I might stick to this outline for only a chapter or two, or I might stay true to its essence until the very end of the book. I might also follow this outline for ten chapters, hit a wall, then create a whole new outline starting from where the flow stopped.

In the course of writing a novel, I may make several outlines, each one a poetic exploration of a possible course of events and character evolution.ॐTW

2. Write a paragraph-long micro-chapter for each of your thirty steps.

3. Read your thirty micro-chapters aloud, in order, as a single work.

4. If you really like what you've created so far, get to work on the novel!

Examples

of

Story

Exercises

Telling Stories—*What Just Happened to You? page 143*

PARTNER EXERCISE (MT)

1 and 2. Tell a story about something that just happened to you; partner jots down key words and phrases.

sarcasm, hippie, attitude toward others, unhappy folks, tofu and broccoli

3. Referring to notes made by partner, write out your story.

Sitting at Dragon House, one of seventeen local Chinese restaurants, I get caught up in the lives of others, as I imagine them. If my assumptions about these strangers are accurate, we are not a happy species.

The couple there by the front window haven't spoken a word to each other. I think she is on the verge of crying or screaming or bolting out the door as he sits ever so coolly staring out the window. The family over there—father, son, son's girlfriend or wife—don't talk much either, and the son's posture, in particular, suggests an expectation of defeat. I am waited upon by the owner's daughter, about thirteen, who responds sarcastically when I order and is rude as another customer pays his bill.

Either the whole world is having a bad day, or I'm making it all up out of my own low vitality. I wonder where I left my rose-colored glasses.

4. Read aloud, then rewrite your story.

I was sitting at Dragon House, one of the cheap local Chinese restaurants, where I had gone to read over my notes on *The Scribbler's Manifesto* before heading to Todd's for a writing session. I had a headache, aftermath of an intense bout of feasting on pasta al pesto, grilled salmon, and Chianti at my neighbor's house the evening before. My focus was definitely off and easily snagged by the lives of my fellow lunch patrons. If my assumptions about these strangers were accurate, we are not a happy species.

The couple by the front window didn't speak a word to each other in the half hour I sat sipping jasmine tea and picking at my tofu and broccoli. Her face told a story of boredom and frustration. I thought she would scream and bolt out the door as he sat staring out the window, coolly ignoring her existence. The trio by the far wall—father, son, son's girlfriend or wife—didn't talk much either, and the son's posture suggested an expectation of defeat. I was waited upon by the daughter of the restaurant's owner, who has developed since I first met her from sweet child to rude and sarcastic teenager.

Either the whole world was having a bad day, or I was making it all up out of my own low vitality. I wish I could find my rose-colored glasses.

PARTNER EXERCISE (TW)

1 and 2. Tell a story about something that just happened to you; partner jots down key words and phrases.

writing book, cookies, walk, coffee, eating

3. Referring to notes made by partner, write out your story.

Mindy and I meet one or two times a week to write together. Today, Mindy arrived wanting coffee. She said her brain was mush from overwork, and since I don't have coffee in the house, we walked around the corner to get some.

At the bakery, along with her cappuccino, we got a couple of cookies. While Mindy waited for her drink, I read the sports section of a discarded newspaper and saw that my beloved Giants had lost to the Dodgers again. Sigh.

Then we walked home and sat down to write, but before we got too far along we took some time to blab about our lives.

4. Read aloud, then rewrite your story.

Mindy, an auspiciously atypical Aries, and I, a double Libra, enjoy writing together about the interconnection of fate and personality. We meet one or two times a week. Each of our meetings is planned to coincide with harmonious astrological indices.

Examples

of

Story

Exercises

Today, Neptune trining Mars, Mindy arrived wanting coffee. She said her brain was mush from overwork, and since I don't have coffee in the house, we walked around the corner to get some at the Aquarian Conspiracy bakery. I felt my Virgo moon fighting hard to overcome the day's heavy Capricorn influences.

At the bakery, along with Mindy's cappuccino, we got a couple of cookies. While Mindy waited for her drink, I read the sports section of a discarded newspaper and saw that my beloved Giants, a Pisces-heavy squad, had lost to the Scorpio-dominated Dodgers again. Sigh.

Then we walked home and sat down to write at 3:07, just as Venus entered Sagittarius. But before we got too far along we took some time to blab about our lives, and to make sure our rising signs were in no danger of colliding.

Telling Stories—*Jokes, Basic Exercise, page 144 (TW)*

SOME HELP

So this guy named Jeremy goes to see a psychiatrist. He lies down on the sofa and talks for an hour, saying whatever comes into his head. When his time is up, the psychiatrist says, "I think you're crazy." Jeremy sits up, deeply offended, and says, "Hey, I want a second opinion." And the psychiatrist says, "Okay, you're ugly, too."

VARIATION 1: Write out the joke, then write what happens to the main character after the joke ends; plus Variation 2: set the joke in another time and place; plus Variation 3: write a similar story that ends differently and isn't necessarily funny.

SOME HELP

Merlin looked out over the castle keep, a dense fog drifting in from the sea. He closed his old eyes and sighed heavily, wondering why it had been such a long time since he'd heard from the spirit realm. It had been months since he'd heard anything of meaning from the wind, and a good year since he'd been able to conjure a reasonably intelligent fairy. He yawned expansively and stroked his wispy white beard. He was weary from a long night of curing baby Arthur's whooping cough, and now he wanted to sleep. Alas, Sir Jeremy was due any minute, and Merlin had promised to help him interpret a troubling dream.

A thunderous knock on the heavy door announced Jeremy's arrival. A moment later, the mighty knight lay sprawled on Merlin's plush purple sofa, babbling about unicorns and witches and leaky chalices. Merlin sat on a high stool by the open window, striving valiantly to listen to Jeremy, yet finding himself wholly disinterested, his mind awash in alchemical equations and bits of lyrics from bawdy drinking songs.

At the end of an hour, Jeremy sat up and said, "Well? What thinkest thou?"

"Madness," said Merlin, opening his eyes. "I believe you are mad."

Angered by the wizard's retort, Jeremy rose to his feet and bellowed, "I shall seek another opinion."

"Seek no further," said Merlin, fearing no man. "Here is another. You resemble a large hog. And another. You have the intelligence of a twice-swatted gnat."

So furious was the mighty Jeremy, that he reached out to throttle the old man, only to find himself flying backwards at a fantastic speed, soaring high above the kingdom and far out over the sea.

"Gads," he said, speaking aloud, for he never thought quietly, "what was I thinking? Merlin is impervious to…well, then so I wasn't thinking, and my temper got the better of me yet again. Oh, dear God, when will I ever learn? Yet weren't his words cruel? Why should he use me so when I came so humbly for help? And now what will befall me?"

Then he heard a voice he knew to be Merlin's. "You will end your flight not far from France," said the wizard. "And should you survive the sharks and reach that dreaded shore, your dream shall become manifest."

"Oh, good," said Jeremy, relaxing for the long flight ahead. "I've always wanted to see a unicorn."

Telling Stories—*Dreams, page 145*

PARTNER EXERCISE

1. Each tells the other a dream. (MT)

Tad and I are on a driving trip, following a mountain road. As we make a sharp right hand turn, we see that many people are standing at a lookout railing, apparently admiring the view. We pull over and park in the shade, then leave the car and join the crowd. The view is of a vast, deep chasm—beautiful—but my eye is caught by something moving off to my right, where a rocky promontory looms high above where we stand. There are some houses on the lower part of the pinnacle, then bare rock juts at least a hundred feet straight upward. I see a man wearing a loincloth climbing the bare rock at superhuman speed. His strength, determination, and focus are awesome. As he approaches the highest point he shows no sign of slowing and I suddenly worry that he intends to throw himself off the mountain into the chasm. My attention is riveted to his rapidly ascending form in the distance. He reaches the top and indeed steps off the rock, but he doesn't fall. I watch, amazed, as he continues striding purposefully across the bright blue sky.

> Key phrases and details: *traveling, mountain, rocky crag, man climbing fast, loincloth, realizing he's not gonna stop when he gets to top, alarmed, worried, fall or jump, continues on toward the heavens*

1. Each tells the other a dream. (TW)

I am crossing an enormous footbridge spanning a wide river or some other large body of water. The bridge is big enough for cars to go across but there are only people walking. Most of the people are just hanging out on the bridge. They don't seem to see me. I am half or two-thirds of the way across when I come to a side bridge. I go down it and find myself in a two-story house with Julie, my ex-wife. I'm uncertain if we live there together or whether we are both just visiting. I go upstairs to have some privacy and the walls of the house begin to disintegrate. The floor becomes transparent. I go downstairs and out the door, leaving Julie behind. I return to the main bridge and continue on my way across the river.

Key phrases and details: *footbridge, wide river, side bridge, Julie, uncertainty, transparent floor, return to main bridge*

2. Each writes a short story combining details from the two dreams. (MT)

The woman stood alone on the footbridge, leaning over the railing, studying the swirling patterns in the brown water that was rushing wildly, loud and littered with debris after the weekend's freak storm.

The old bridge swayed a little in the strong evening wind and she felt a morbid thrill as she imagined the possibility of the splintered boards beneath her feet suddenly giving way. The thought that she might be plunged into the river and caught up in its blind racing to the sea terrified her, but the terror made her feel more alive than she had in months.

Since Caitlin's death she had had no idea where her life was going, or why it was continuing at all. Who was she if not a mother? The impassive yet purposeful drive of the swollen river seemed to call her awake somehow.

That morning, feeling restless after her second cup of strong black coffee, she had dressed warmly against the weather and set out walking with determination, desperate to discover some reason to care again about life, some path that might ignite her interest and imagination. And the fates had led her to this treacherous bridge spanning a powerful river. Surely there was some important message for her in this place. She had taken to looking everywhere for messages and signs, scanning the inner and outer landscapes for hints of meaning.

She heard the man before she saw him, calling out a primitive chant in a language she had never heard. Following the sound, she spotted him—an old brown-skinned man in a loincloth moving along the water's edge, leaping nimbly from rock to rock, hollering out his sing-song prayer as if someone, a god perhaps, was sure to be listening.

The woman's heart thumped hard against her breastbone as she watched his sure-footed pilgrimage along the riverbank. Here was the guide she'd been waiting for.

2. Each writes a story combining details from the two dreams. (TW)

I was on foot, traveling east, traveling alone. I came to a vast river spanned by a wide, sturdy footbridge. I was surprised to find so many other people on the bridge. I'd come to believe the country largely unpopulated. Most of the people were standing or sitting, as if they lived there on the bridge. No one spoke to me, but I felt no unfriendliness from anyone.

Across the river, a mountain rose precipitously from the plains, capped by a fantastic crag of bright gray granite. My eye was drawn by a flash of red against the browns and greens of the mountainside. A man was climbing the mountain, moving with great, purposeful strides. He wore only a red loincloth, his unruly brown hair tumbling to his shoulders.

So mesmerized was I by his amazingly swift ascent, I was unaware at first that the bridge was breaking up beneath me, the planks dissolving as if they were being melted away by the sun. In a panic, I ran across the bridge, leaping to the eastern shore just as the few remaining fragments of the bridge fell into the roaring current.

No one else had crossed with me. I scanned the waters for survivors but saw none. Had they all perished? Had they fled to the other side?

I turned away from the river and looked toward the mountain, searching the slope for the climber. To my astonishment, he was nearly to the top of the crowning crag, yet he was not slowing.

A sense of dread overcame me. I was certain he meant to leap to his death. My instinct was to close my eyes to spare myself the horror of his fall, but some force greater than my will compelled me to keep my eyes open and fixed on him.

He reached the top and strode unhesitatingly to the edge. I wanted to shout, "No! Don't do it! Don't throw your precious life away!" But no words would come.

He strode into space, but did not fall. He continued to climb through the sky, held aloft by the firmament of miracles.

Earliest Memories—*Basic Exercise, page 146 (TW)*

1 and 2. While consciously remembering your past, write a list of seven things or events.

1. Casey cat – rat on garbage can
2. Mary – our cleaning lady – I scared her, she swatted me
3. Mother weeding succulents
4. Poking holes in screen with pencil – Texas
5. My dad saying, "Say when," pouring milk
6. First fish – hot park, Texas
7. Getting lost in store – army base – found by black man

3. Spontaneously choose one of the items.

    Poking holes in screen with pencil – Texas

4. Write down some details surrounding this memory.

    Screened porch – multi-storied building – bored, hot, Texas, bugs are enemy, no punishment, striped shirt, new baby, workmen replacing screen, shame

5. Write an account of the memory in first person, present tense.

I am four-and-a-half. I'm wearing blue shorts and a shirt with black and white stripes. I mostly go barefoot. It is very hot in Texas, where we live. My mom just came home from the hospital with my new brother. They said I would have a playmate now but he's still too little. I put a ball in his crib but he didn't see it.

We live in a big building. Four stories. My dad is a captain in the Army. Fort Sam Houston. All around every apartment is a big, screened porch. This is where we sleep on hot summer nights. If the screens were gone the bugs would eat us alive.

Sometimes I get bored. My mother doesn't have any time

for me now and my dad's at work. My sisters have other friends. There aren't other boys to play with. That's why they got my brother, but he's too little. He can't even walk yet. Or even sit up.

Anyway, I take a pencil and poke its tip into the screen and push, and it makes a wonderful sound—like a whisper—and makes a perfect round little hole. So I keep doing it. Over and over again.

But now my mom sees it, all the holes, and she says, "Why did you do this? Now the bugs will eat us alive!"

So she calls the men and they come to fix it. One old man looks at the holes, and now he looks at me and says, "You do that?"

I start to cry and run away, but I come back to watch them take out the old screen and put in the new one. I want to poke more holes, but I won't.

Earliest Memories—*Basic Exercise, page 146 (MT)*

1 and 2. While consciously remembering your past, write a list of seven things or events.

1. Nursery bed
2. Dill pickles on sticks – Germany
3. Aunt Greta's Oz books
4. Camping at Lake Almanor
5. Brother Bill being bitten by a duck
6. Falling into an icy ditch on my way to school
7. Hanging upside down on a metal bar

3. Spontaneously choose one of the items.

    Aunt Greta's Oz books

4. Write down some details surrounding this memory.

    Beautifully illustrated books, kept in attic, used to be cousin Jane's (who's now grown up), fantasy world, ladder to attic, lust for those books and the piano, the stable life with enough money, envy

5. Write an account of the memory in first person, present tense.

I love those Oz books, with their bright and fanciful illustrations, the books that are cousin Jane's, though she's grown up and in college and probably doesn't ever think about them anymore. I love climbing the ladder through the crawlspace in my Aunt Greta's closet, into the attic where the trunk is kept that holds those precious books. I always ask to see them, Aunt Greta usually says yes, and ordinary reality disappears for a while as I slowly turn the big pages, poring with new delight over words and drawings I have studied dozens of times before.

I don't just love those books, I want to own them. I want to own the Oz books, and the piano, and the house that is clean and pretty and peaceful, and the backyard with its apple tree and grape vines and lush, cool lawn.

I want the life my cousin Jane had growing up affluent, but I'd settle for the books. I think Aunt Greta senses all this, and she loves me and would like to please me, but she can't quite let loose of those old books.

So I grow up, and eventually come to feel blessed because I understand that happiness doesn't depend on owning things. I come to feel so grateful for my poor but generous mother, who laughed and sang and kissed me every day.

Arbitrary Story Structures—*Basic Exercise, two different short stories generated from Arbitrary Story Structure 6, page 150*

EVERYBODY ELSE
by Todd

You are sitting somewhere having a favorite drink.

I was sitting on my back porch sipping a strawberry milkshake and watching the chickadees swarming the bird feeder when out of the sycamore came a big ornery jay to scatter the little birds and hog all the food. I told myself not to take sides, not to think the little birds were good, the big bully bird bad, but I couldn't help it. I identified with the little guys and I have no fondness for bullies.

You remember something your mother said to you and the circumstances surrounding her saying it.

I got beat up by several different bullies when I was in elementary school. I wasn't much of a fighter, but I frequently came to the aid of smaller kids being knocked around by bigger kids. One hot summer day, my mother was nursing the bloody nose I got from putting myself between little Billy Breeden and big Mike Wotila, and she said, "Simon, you just may be too good for this world." She'd never said anything like that to me before, and never did again, so it stuck in my mind, and I thought about it over the years, and I came to believe she was telling me, in her sweet way, to mind my own business.

Someone approaches and speaks to you.

Then Roger called to me over the side fence. He and his wife Cecily, and their son Aubrey, were my neighbors to the north. "Hey, Simon," he said, "you gonna watch the fight? My television blew a fuse or something."

You answer them and a conversation ensues.

"What fight?" I said, wishing he hadn't interrupted my thoughts of my mother. It wasn't often I thought of her.

"*What* fight?" he said, sneering at me. "You gotta be kidding. *The* fight. The heavyweight championship of the world. Should be awesome. Monster heavy hitters."

"I…Roger, I don't have a television. And if I did, I wouldn't watch a fight. I…"

Then I heard him say to someone, "He says he doesn't *have* a television. I told you he doesn't like me."

You are walking somewhere, thinking about the person you had the conversation with.

I decided to go over and talk to him, to explain why I didn't have a television. I didn't want him to think I was snubbing him. So I put my milkshake in the fridge, went out the front door, down the steps and over to Roger and Cecily's. Their yard was a mess. Roger drank heavily. Cecily yelled at him to mow the lawn but he usually didn't. I mowed it for them once a month if he didn't get to it.

You remember something about the conversation.

Funny, but what stuck in my mind was not that Roger said I didn't like him, or that he implied by his tone that he thought I *did* have a television and was lying so I wouldn't have to spend time with him. No, what stuck in my mind was the expression, "You gotta be kidding." I realized more profoundly than ever before that people—men, women, teachers, friends, everybody—had been saying "You gotta be kidding" to me all my life. And I realized I was fed up with people doubting me.

You find something in your path that answers a question.

At which moment I bumped into Aubrey, Roger and Cecily's eleven-year-old son, an odd little boy I often saw playing by himself. He looked so very sad. "Are you okay, Aubrey?"

He looked up at me, smiling bravely through his tears, and said, "Oh, *I'm* okay, even if somebody else doesn't think so."

A THERMOS OF TEA
by Mindy

You are sitting somewhere having a favorite drink.

Fine Pearl Jasmine is, in my humble opinion, the best tea in the world, and I've sampled hundreds of varieties, so I know what I'm talking about. At two hundred dollars a pound it's not for everyone, I realize, but those of us who can afford it should consider it among the true joys of affluence.

You remember something your mother said to you and the circumstances surrounding her saying it.

This bench on the lawn in front of the main library is my favorite spot on sunny mornings. I feel relaxed and happy here, sipping expensive tea, considering how very right for me is the life of the tenured professor of humanities. My mother, of course, understands perfectly why I didn't go into medicine, my father's plan for me. "He's an ass," she often assured me as we dawdled over lunch at Sardino's. "Listen to him and you're doomed."

Someone approaches and speaks to you.

My eye drifts to the bike path that runs along the creek, and I watch as a cyclist approaches the library. The bike is heavily burdened. There are bulging saddlebags and a large wooden box strapped to the rear. The bike is pulling a small trailer, packed, it appears, for a camping trip, with sleeping bag and propane stove.

"Hello," calls the cyclist, "what school is this?"

You answer them and a conversation ensues.

"The University of California," I answer politely.

"What city is this?"

I can't help raising my eyebrows in astonishment. "Berkeley," I reply.

You are walking somewhere, thinking about the person you had the conversation with.

I replace the lid on my thermos of tea and walk off toward my first lecture of the day. It's early yet, but I simply have no desire to engage in conversation with a person who apparently finds being a vagabond appealing in some way. It worries me, when I occasionally consider such things, that there are people who don't know or seem to care where they are or what they're doing at any given time.

You remember something about the conversation.

What city, indeed! I am fairly certain that man is not college-educated. Why, he's probably not even a taxpayer!

I am walking more quickly than usual, feeling overheated and, yes, I admit it, irritated that my morning ritual should be disturbed by such a person. Security measures should be taken on campus. I am a firm believer that a safe and uncluttered environment is essential for serious study.

You find something in your path that answers a question.

Something gleams from the edge of the walkway, a glint of gold metal. I bend down and pick it up—an earring, a heart with a small diamond at its center. My God! It's Elizabeth's. I had them made for her last Christmas!

How long has it lain there—surely not more than a day on this busy path. So she *has* come back.

Inventing Your Own Structures: Random Structures—
Basic Exercise, Partner Writing, page 154 (TW/MT)

Co-created Random Structure: *Falling, Listening, Flower, Grandmother, Song*

FALLING

The night the sky fell, I became a new person. I had never before witnessed a meteor shower, and lying on my back in Sylvia's pasture, with Timothy beside me on a patchwork blanket, I gave myself to the cosmos, to god, you might say, for the first time in my life. (MT)

LISTENING

Timothy was snoring his little baby snore, and in my reverie he sounded like a part of the river. You know how a river makes a roar or a gurgle or some single sound at first hearing, but then if you listen carefully you can hear separate parts of the larger sound. That's what was happening to me in my moment of opening. The parts were revealing themselves, and Timothy's breath was a part of the river. (TW)

FLOWER

I thought of peonies, their luscious blossoming after the long wait, and of the lesser (though still beautiful) flowers that surrender themselves all spring and summer, without hesitation, to some inner urging, a drive to express their true nature. (MT)

GRANDMOTHER

What was it Granny said to all of us a moment before her dying, her eyes brimming with light—a light that made her tears seem solid and edible? "I can see the falls, but there is no danger." At least that's what I heard, but in the meadow, aroused and open and blissfully connected, I understood she'd been saying, "Heed the call. No danger." Beyond the literal, under the last gasp, I'm sure she was urging us to open. (TW)

SONG

I thought of all kinds of things out there in the darkness, with the universe exploding above me. I thought of Don and Melissa, how they willfully stopped loving each other; of my first pony, Pearl, and her exquisite eyes caressing me; of old Mr. Garcia who drank tequila and told me stories as we harvested tomatoes side-by-side in the fields west of Fresno. But mostly I thought of Timothy and me, our journey together that was just beginning, and how in some way I could never describe, we both belonged to the song of the stars. (MT)

Diagramming the Structures of Favorite Books and Stories—*Basic Exercise, page 159*

The Original Story:

THE BIG GREEN
by Todd

I've always been weird. In first grade, I would stand barefoot by a tree at the far end of the playground, and I could feel the stories coming up through the earth into my feet, and traveling up my legs and through my heart and out my mouth into the air. At first, the other kids laughed at me, but I simply *had* to do it. Every recess, I would run to the tree, pull off my shoes and start babbling.

I didn't have a single friend when I first started telling the stories, but one day this little boy sat down nearby and listened to me for a few minutes. Then he got up and ran away, returning a moment later with four other kids, and pretty soon *they* got up and ran away and came back with more kids, and I just kept telling my story of the three children lost in a mysterious forest called the Big Green. And pretty soon there were hundreds of kids sitting around me in concentric circles, and when the bell rang, none of them would budge until I said The End.

Well, from then on I had all sorts of friends, and my teacher invited me to tell stories to the class while she took little naps, and pretty soon I was going to other classrooms full of older kids, and I'd tell them stories, too, until finally I was named the official storyteller of the school, and I was interviewed and photographed for the school paper, and then for the local newspaper, which is when my mother and father found out about it.

I'll never forget that night. It was a week or so before my seventh birthday. My father came home from his office, and my mother showed him the article about me, and he became quite upset. "What are all these stories *about?*" he wanted to know.

I told him they were mostly about lost children, and he said, *"You've* never been lost. How can you make up stories about things you don't know about?" Big pause, fierce frown. "That's *lying.*"

"They're just stories," I said, trying to defend myself. "They like us to make up stories."

"Who likes you to?"

"The teachers."

"Why didn't you *tell* us about this?" He glared at my mother. "Did *you* know about this?"

"Heavens no," she said, rolling her eyes. "He doesn't tell me anything."

"So now all our friends are gonna see this and. . ."

"We've had five calls already."

"Great," said my father, clenching his fists. "That does it. No more storytelling. You hear me? No more."

"But. . ."

"But nothing. If I hear about you telling another story, lying again, you'll be in big big trouble."

So I stopped. It was a difficult time for me. I lost most of my new friends, and I got beat up a few times by older kids trying to force me to tell them stories, but I'd been in big big trouble with my father before, and it wasn't something I would risk again until I was much older.

I hadn't remembered any of this until last year when I went to a psychic astrologer to celebrate turning forty-three, and the first thing he said to me was, "Your greatest gift emerged when you were six, but something happened and you were forced to squelch it."

"Gift?" I said, remembering only my profound loneliness. "Like what?"

He squinted at my chart. "You were, perhaps, psychic, and judging from the way your moon conjuncts Mars, I would imagine that such a gift would have been largely unacceptable in your family."

"I don't remember," I said, straining for any sort of image from those years.

"And then you turned to the physical. Sports?"

"It's all I did," I said, remembering the endless baseball, the safe simplicity of the bat meeting the ball, drifting back in left field to catch another towering drive, never ever wanting the day to end.

"And now?"

"I work at a preschool. I'm a teacher's aide."

Then it hit me, the way I keep the kids entertained between four and six, waiting for their mommies to come pick them up. I stand by a tree at the far end of the playground and tell them stories about the two boys and the little girl lost in the Big Green. Only now that I've remembered how it all began, I make sure to take my shoes off.

The Abstract Structure of "The Big Green"

Part 1. Alienation

Part 2. Acceptance

Part 3. Acclaim

Part 4. Suspicion

Part 5. Anger

Part 6. Forbidden

Part 7. Astrologer

Part 8. Gift

Part 9. Sport

Part 10. Rediscovery

The Arbitrary Story Structure of "The Big Green"

Part 1. Someone feels alienated

Part 2. He does something to change his situation

Part 3. He receives support for making a change

Part 4. Someone is suspicious of the person's success

Part 5. An argument ensues

Part 6. Something becomes forbidden

Part 7. A fortuneteller is consulted

Part 8. A gift is given

Part 9. A game is played

Part 10. Something long lost is rediscovered

A new story modeled on the structure of "The Big Green"

FORTUNE
by Mindy

Someone feels alienated.

Dudley sat sullenly in an uncomfortable chair near a tacky fountain on the hotel veranda. He could hear bad pop tunes booming from the banquet hall where his twentieth high-school reunion was in full swing. He had never before attended one of these forced frolics with people who were somewhat familiar but not at all interesting. He had come this time because of a feeling, a certain sensation in or around his solar plexus, that felt like a premonition. Dudley had recently decided to develop his spiritual side and so was following such urgings whenever possible. He had actually believed that something fortuitous was destined to happen at this reunion. But at this moment, bored to distraction, he found all that preposterous. He must be losing his grip on reality!

They do something to change their situation.

In mid-grumble, Dudley stood up and strode into the banquet hall, having just remembered his therapist lecturing him on Tuesday about his tendency to stew in negativity, endlessly pronouncing judgment on life.

They receive support for making a change.

His eyes had barely adjusted to the dimmed lights of the room when he thought he heard a voice whispering his name. "Dudley!" There it was again, sounding urgent. He spun around in annoyance, but also with a stirring of curiosity. He had intended to remain aloof and anonymous all evening, as he had throughout high school, but apparently someone had recognized him. Despite himself, he was pleased to no longer feel invisible and utterly alone.

Someone is suspicious of the person's success.

"What? Who is that?" he whispered back into the darkness.

"It's Valerie Pakowski."

She stood directly in front of him now, barely visible in the darkness, like a phantom from his past. He again felt that strange stirring behind his navel. "Valerie," he repeated, suddenly remembering the frustrated longing he had felt for this person throughout his junior and senior years. She had spoken to him rarely but suggestively, flounced her hair when she knew he was watching, and he could swear she even winked at him once or twice, basically teasing him to the point of maudlin misery.

"Listen," she said now. "Is that limousine out front waiting for you?"

"What?" Dudley said, stalling for time. He was being deluged with disconcerting memories at the moment but finally decided he could handle this simple question. "Yes."

"I don't believe it," Valerie snorted. "I heard you were a starving artist!"

An argument ensues.

The sensation in Dudley's stomach was becoming more pronounced, and it wasn't hunger. He hoped he was not about to belch, or worse. "Valerie, I'm sure you think you know all about my life," he said snootily to take his mind off the nausea, "but the fact is you know absolutely nothing." He liked the feel of this bit of sarcastic truth-telling, and decided to tell some more. "People are always mistaking their puny interpretations of reality for reality itself!"

Valerie blinked at him for a moment, then said snidely, "Well, you certainly don't know a damn thing about my assumptions and interpretations. You're not at this very moment assuming anything about me, are you?"

Something becomes forbidden.

He was, in fact, assuming at that moment that Valerie was flirting with him. He had always been intuitive, and right then he knew in his bones that this conversation was merely the first act in a lengthy play, a teasing prelude to something extremely direct and probably enjoyable. In his rapture at the thought that Valerie might finally be his, Dudley stepped closer to her and lifted her hand impulsively to his lips. "Valerie, you're lovely by strobe light," he said.

She jerked her hand away as if his lips had burned her. "Don't touch me," she snarled, but she didn't walk away. Apparently, Valerie Pakowski still enjoyed playing cat and mouse. It was a game at which Dudley, too, had become skilled. Such was love in these times.

A fortuneteller is consulted.

A break in the music was being announced. Dudley spoke to Valerie with what he hoped resembled a sexy sneer. "Would you like to see the inside of my limo?" Having thus enticed her—sufficiently, he hoped—he turned on his heels and sauntered—seductively, he hoped—from the banquet room into the main corridor of the hotel. He glanced over his shoulder to see if Valerie was indeed following him toward the main lobby, like a lemming drawn irresistibly to the sea, but she was veering off in the direction of a table draped in vivid red and gold fabric that sat against the wall at the end of the corridor. A banner above the table proclaimed, "Madame Melody's Crystal Ball." Then, in smaller letters, "Class of 1974. I know your past. Now let me tell your future."

Valerie glanced around at Dudley and beckoned him with a hooked finger and a strange little smile. Reluctant but intrigued, he made his way to her side. "Madame Melody says she can read our future," Valerie said. "For five dollars."

Had he heard right? Had Valerie said "our" future? Apparently she assumed they would have one together, which caused his stomach to recommence its strange convulsions. Couldn't they just have wild and crazy sex and leave it at that? As a younger man, he had desperately wanted a soulmate, a partner, a compatible companion to grace his days forever, but the circumstances of his life had caused him to reject this ideal as a pipe dream. He had grown accustomed to his uncommitted life, punctuated by pleasurable but not at all demanding physical encounters, and was not sure any more that he wanted anything different.

"I'll pay ten dollars for two fortunes," Dudley said, groping for his wallet. "One for her and one for me."

A gift is given.

"Please," said Madame Melody, gazing at Dudley mysteriously through thick fake eyelashes. "For yours, there is no charge." Dudley stared. This exotic woman wearing too much make-up looked vaguely familiar. His mind went rummaging through his high school experiences for some clue to her identity. Within several seconds it came to him.

"Charlene?" Dudley said, his eyes widening. "Charlene Sawyer? You look so different in a turban!"

"I am Madame Melody now," she said. "The past is dead."

A game is played.

"The past is dead?" Dudley repeated. Personally, he felt that the past was still very much alive and tenacious as a bulldog, harassing him constantly with regrets and recriminations. "I don't see how you can say such a thing."

"Forgiveness is freedom," said Madame Melody, and Dudley suddenly remembered playing chess with Charlene Sawyer after school most afternoons when they were both seniors and founding members of the Chess Club. He had barely noticed her as a person—they played silently and his mind was usually on Valerie—but she was a formidable adversary on the board. He enjoyed their games, during which she anticipated his plays like a mind reader, but their relationship had ended at graduation without so much as a farewell.

"Would you like to have dinner with me tomorrow?" he heard himself asking.

"Why should I?" said Valerie haughtily.

"Not you, Valerie," Dudley said without turning. The eyes of the fortuneteller had a ferocious grip on his own. "I am speaking to Madame Melody."

The fortuneteller's face smiled up at him without a trace of guile, framed with dark ringlets and gold and crystal earrings. "And perhaps a game of chess?" she said.

The following evening and for countless evenings thereafter, Dudley and Charlene sat quietly over cups of Darjeeling in Dudley's humble loft apartment (the rented limo had been a pretense he could ill afford). Between kisses, they moved marble chess pieces around on a board, listened to Louis and Ella doing the great jazz standards, and never once talked of the past.

Stories from Visuals: Stories from a Single Image—
Basic Exercise, page 160 (MT)

A story inspired by the photograph.

CHLOE

They say water is the essence of life. For me this is true. Since childhood I've floated down rivers, rowed across lakes, and bodysurfed in the vast, pulsing Pacific at every opportunity. Wherever there is water, especially big water, I am happy.

Clearly my daughter, Chloe, is like me in this. She owns all the toys and books and games ever created for a one-year-old—gifts from the two adoring grandmothers and seven cooing aunts who swarm continually around my only child—but Chloe prefers the garden hose. I set up my easel and paint for hours every morning while she romps naked in the sun, dragging along the magical green tube that pours forth "wah-doo"—her first and, so far, only word, and she always pronounces it rapturously.

Brian says I'm irresponsible, just letting the faucet run like that—a waste of our precious natural resources, he says. Less of a waste than television, I reply, which he watches at least three hours every evening. Plus he goes through toilet paper by the truckload and he's addicted to Diet Coke. Is this the behavior of a true environmentalist?

Anyway, Chloe and I are moving on in a few weeks, leaving Brian to his vices, taking up residence for the winter in Costa Rica, where people understand about art and solitude and naked baby bliss, and where water is considered a goddess, beautiful and powerful and essential in a way maybe only Chloe and I, of all norte Americanos, understand.

Stories from Visuals: Stories from a Single Image—
Variation 4, a story in which the photograph depicts the final scene, page 160 (TW)

TRUTH

I was at Miriam's house this morning. Miriam used to be my wife, but we found, after six difficult years, that life was better for both of us if we kept a good distance between us. We live in neighboring towns now, and we've been seeing each other a few times a year. She remarried, I have not. We moved apart two years ago. She was forty-seven, I was forty-nine. Eight months after I moved out, Miriam had a baby. A boy. She claims I'm the father. I wish I believed her.

The guy she married, Stan, thinks he's the father, which he may be. Miriam says she lets him think that so he'll be a better father, but she knows he's not. Mathematically impossible. Or so she says. I've never been able to trust Miriam, about anything, which is why our marriage was doomed. Stan, on the other hand, believes everything she says. I could call him a fool, but I'd have to say he's a happy fool. Or maybe I'm the fool.

So Miriam has a baby. His name is Philip. He's fifteen months old and I love him. I didn't want to love him because I didn't want to feel tied to Miriam in any way. She broke my heart so many times I thought I was going to die. But the minute I saw him, I loved him.

Why don't I think he's my kid? Because Miriam and I stopped making love a year or so before I moved out. She claims there was the one last time, our farewell dance she calls it, and that's when Philip was conceived. Except I remember the dance, and how sad I was to feel so disconnected, so already gone, so not with her. And I stopped before I could have made a child. At least I thought I did. I've told her this, but she says it can only be me. There were no others until Stan came along, a good two months into her pregnancy.

So this morning I get to Miriam's right after Stan leaves for work. Phil is in his high-chair squealing and laughing and banging his spoon, food splattered everywhere, his face smeared with mooshed bananas and mashed potatoes.

Miriam says to me, "Take him out back and hose him off. I gotta go to the bathroom."

I pick him up and he gurgles in delight. He really likes me. I take him out on the little lawn and set him down by the hose. He squats there looking at the hose end, his eyes wide with curiosity. Then he looks up at me and nods. I cross the brick patio and turn on the hose, and the water gushes out into the grass. Then he very carefully picks up the hose with his right hand and rinses off his left hand. Then he switches hands and rinses off his right. And then he holds the hose in both hands and bows his head into the stream, washing the food from his face.

Miriam and I could never agree about anything. She believed in God, I didn't. She trusted complete strangers, I couldn't trust my own mother. But when she comes up beside me and puts her arm around my waist, and we watch Philip communing with the water, I feel like I'm watching a spirit being who has just incarnated into a human body. I feel I am in the presence of divine truth.

Beginnings: The First Sentence—*Basic Exercise, page 164 (MT)*

1. Quickly write a first sentence.

Duncan dangled his feet lazily in the hotel fountain.

2 and 3. Finish paragraph; select key sentence.

Duncan dangled his feet lazily in the hotel fountain. He had taken his shoes off with a great sigh and now swabbed at his neck with a handkerchief as the pulsing ache in his legs began to subside. **Doris knew he hated the tramping thing,** but she had insisted on dragging him all over Rome in the midday heat.

4 and 5. Write new paragraph beginning with selected sentence; select key word.

Doris knew Duncan hated the tramping thing, but she wanted him with her—for **protection**, she supposed. She had dragged him all over Rome in the midday heat and now he sat red-faced on the hotel veranda, swabbing at his thick neck with an already soiled handkerchief. Doris could see he was not a happy man.

6. Write first sentence containing key word; finish paragraph.

Doris desired protection, so she had dragged Duncan all over Rome in the midday heat. He knew the city could be dangerous for unaccompanied females—the life force in these Latin men was so strong—so he went along. But he resented her for insisting on tramping endlessly along narrow streets in the old part of town, where every building looked almost exactly like the last. Doris saw something new and exciting at every turn. Herein lay the primary difference between them, and it was enough to spoil everything.

Beginnings: The First Sentence—*First Sentences, Variation 2, page 164 (TW)*

Each opening line begins an entirely new story.

1. Quickly write a first sentence.

Gerald had no idea where he was.

2 and 3. Finish paragraph; select key sentence.

Gerald had no idea where he was. He remembered going into the movie theater, finding his seat, watching the trailers. He remembered the movie starting—fog drifting by a castle on a treeless plain. But then what had happened? He couldn't remember. He only knew that now **he was on a treeless plain, dense fog swirling around him**.

4 and 5. Write new paragraph beginning with selected sentence; select key word.

He was on a treeless plain, dense fog swirling around him. He had come there hoping for a clear day. He wanted to take a picture that showed clearly how the cliff was virtually **imperceptible**, even when the sun was shining. Without the picture his boss would never believe he'd wrecked the truck completely by accident.

6. Write first sentence containing key word; finish paragraph.

"Don't be crazy," said Dana, sneering at me. "That pimple is imperceptible."

"How can it be imperceptible," I groaned, "if you can see it to says it's imperceptible?"

Dana sighed and shook her head. I knew what she was going to say. It's what she always says after she sighs and shakes her head that way: "Marvin, I pity you. I really do."

Beginnings: The First Page—*Basic Exercise, page 165 (TW)*

1. Write the first page of a story.

Mary was beautiful and that's what people said about her when they spoke of meeting her. "Wasn't she beautiful?" Then they would quickly add something else to their assessment, as if they were embarrassed to be so taken with her appearance. "And so nice," they would say. Or "And quite bright, too."

She was nice, and exceedingly bright, but her beauty was so pronounced, so loud, as it were, few people ever heard or felt anything over the din of her gorgeous face, her glinting green eyes, her preposterous grace.

Mary was well aware of her impact on people. For a time as a teenager, and then in college, she tried to obfuscate her beauty by wearing formless clothes, ugly coiffures, and garish glasses, though her eyesight was perfect. All to no avail. Her beauty burst all bounds, rendered all disguises moot.

And so she stopped trying to hide herself and vowed to marry the first man who could see past her beauty and into her heart of hearts. She waited seventeen years, became a master chef, a renowned restaurateur, and a respected photojournalist. Then, feeling the cacophonous ticking of her biological clock, she decided to forego marriage and have a child with her friend Maurice, who was blind.

2. Write another first page, beginning the same story again.

Mary was beautiful. The third word she learned to speak was "booful" because she'd heard it so often from everyone she'd ever met.

Until fourth grade all the boys at school said they loved her, and most of the girls did, too. But thereafter her beauty separated her from her peers, breeding resentment and jealousy in those who couldn't help comparing themselves to her.

In the seventh grade, Mary began to wear big-framed glasses, though her eyesight was perfect. She took to ratting her hair and covering her face with gobs of makeup. She wore baggy pants, oversized men's shirts, and truly ugly hats, all to hide her beautiful body and face, all to no avail.

At sixteen she gave up the masquerade and began to dress as she pleased, in the style of a Romanian Gypsy—long skirts and colorful blouses—her face free of makeup, her dark brown hair worn in braids. She stopped traffic.

At nineteen she moved to San Francisco to study cooking at the Morrison Culinary Academy. She'd been offered a full scholarship to Harvard in mathematics, but she longed to be in a place where her beauty would be less of an obstacle to her freedom and comfort. She settled in a neighborhood inhabited almost exclusively by gay men. Within a few weeks they had made her their queen.

3. Write another first page, beginning the same story again.

"It took me a long time to come to terms with my beauty," said Mary, pouring our tea, her voice quiet and clear—a pleasing soprano. "I thank God my parents made so little mention of it. Still, everyone else did."

"You were besieged by men," I said, feeling certain I would

have been among her besiegers had I met her at a different time in our lives.

She sat down in her armchair by the south-facing window and turned to gaze out into the quiet street. She was undeniably gorgeous. Her profile in the diffuse morning light was that of an elemental goddess.

"I was never *seen* by anyone," she said softly. "What they besieged was an illusion, a quirk of genetics, an accidental amalgam of features." She turned to me and squinted. "A mask."

"The Tibetan Buddhists say that one who has been incredibly generous and kind over the course of their life is often reborn a beautiful woman or a handsome man."

"Then I was too kind," she said, laughing. "Shall we change the subject?"

"Yes," I said, infected by her laughter. "How is your boy?"

"Fine," she said, her face softening, her body relaxing. "He's just started seventh grade. Last night he told me he wants to be the first person to win the Indianapolis 500 driving an electric car."

Interview to Create a Story—*Partner Writing, page 166 (TW/MT)*

How did you get here from there?
I was going to take a boat, but then I met a guy who wanted to try walking it. So we walked. It took six years, four of which I spent in a Mexican prison. Next time, I'll fly.

What were you charged with?
Espionage. Incredible. Now my advice to travelers is, "Leave the camcorder at home!"

Mexican prisons have a horrible reputation, yet you say you had a positive experience, overall. Please explain.
Well, the prison, once you've bribed the guard and arranged for sufficient protection (thank god for credit cards), is like a bizarre kind of post-apocalyptic village. I fell in love with a

wonderful woman and learned to weave baskets and make really good tortillas. Staying physically clean was the most daunting challenge. I wrote sixteen screenplays. It was just the break I needed.

So you're back now. What next?
Who knows? Who ever knows? I'm taking things one day at a time. Still making and eating tortillas daily; that's become an important ritual for me. And I'm planting a garden.

Examples

of

Story

Exercises

Chapter Seven

$\mathcal{T}$HE WRITING GROUP

Real learning comes about when the competitive spirit has ceased.

—J. KRISHNAMURTI

Because of the enormous interest in writing today, you should have little trouble assembling a number of people who want to belong to a writing group. An announcement at your place of work or worship, a flyer mailed to friends, or a few strategic phone calls should do the trick. If you have only yourself and one or two friends to start with, that's fine. Word will spread.

There are, of course, many different kinds of writing groups and many different ways for writers to work together. Some groups focus only on poetry or play writing or fiction or writing memoirs. Other groups spend a great deal of time analyzing and criticizing members' work. Still other groups focus on how to get published.

The kind of group we have assembled and facilitated dozens of times is dedicated to practicing various aspects of the writing process through the use of free-writing and the exercises contained in this book. Writers at all levels of experience—raw amateur to polished professional—have benefited from these processes and the synergetic magic of the group experience.

SUGGESTIONS AND CAUTIONS

- We believe nonjudgment and mutual respect to be at the heart of successful group practice. Criticism in a group setting breeds resentment, competition, and comparison. In such a negative atmosphere, members become inhibited about sharing their writing, and more sensitive members will simply withdraw.

- Limit the size of your group to eight members. A larger group greatly diminishes intimacy and focus and creates a classroom atmosphere than can discourage free expression.

- Group members must be committed to regular attendance. Members who attend erratically can diffuse, distract, and even derail the energy of the group process.

- Begin by meeting once every two weeks. You can try meeting every week, but be prepared to shift to every two weeks if interest or commitment lags.

- No homework! Requiring writing outside the group session throws most members into a "back in school" mindset that can undermine their sense of maturity and self-motivation.

- Limit your writing session to roughly two hours, with a break somewhere in the middle. Begin as close to the announced starting time as possible.

- Discourage latecomers. There is nothing more distracting and disruptive to the group process than for someone to arrive after the writing session is underway. After years of seeking a solution to this problem, we instituted the rule: If you're going to be more than ten minutes late, don't come. This solved a myriad of problems.

- At the end of each session, designate a leader for the next meeting. This person will be in charge of choosing the exercises and activities for the next session. She will also facilitate the meeting by introducing exercises and timing them when appropriate. Unless you choose to have a permanent facilitator, rotating this position keeps the group energy

I once led a group in which one of the members sneered whenever she didn't like what another member had written. I spoke to her privately about this habit, but because it was unconscious she couldn't stop herself. Though nonverbal, her facial reactions were quite noticeable and sufficient to inhibit a number of the writers. I had to remove her permanently from the group, after which there was an enormous increase in our enthusiasm and creativity.✌TW

The Fatal Sneer

fresh and eliminates Now-What-Do-We-Do?-itis, which can quickly kill the momentum of a session.

- Analysis and commentary about the writing shared in a group slows the creative process, alienates some members, and selects for people who prefer talking about writing to actually writing. Make it a stated policy that out-loud reactions will be limited to brief, positive comments.

- Doing a few exercises thoroughly at any given meeting is more satisfying and meaningful than doing many exercises quickly.

- Have fun. When the group energy begins to lag, try some Circle Writing or play a game. (We include two detailed descriptions of group word games at the end of this chapter; see pages 208–211.)

- Physical Necessities:
  - Comfortable seating
  - Good light
  - Sufficient heat
  - Minimal distractions (i.e. noise and superfluous activity)

- We recommend that members who wish to share outside work with the group make copies and hand them out to members at the end of a group session. If the writer wants feedback, it can be provided by telephone or at a private meeting.

The First Meeting
(a possible scenario)

The leader (at least for this first meeting) makes sure everyone knows the time and place to meet and instructs them to bring two pens and a notebook. Emphasize the importance of being on time.

When all are comfortably seated, and the temperature of the room is agreeable to everyone, the leader gives an introductory speech that goes something like this.

> Welcome to our group. The first thing I want you to know is that this group will focus on writing rather than on analysis or judgment. In fact, there won't be any criticism of the writing we do in this group. Basic philosophy: If you can't say something nice, don't say anything.
>
> All reading aloud will be voluntary. If we're going around the circle reading what we've created and you don't want to read, just say "Pass." There will never be any pressure on you to read aloud.
>
> There won't be any homework either, except for all the writing you'll be doing on your own because you're so inspired by the positive experience of being in this group. If you want to share something you write outside the group, make copies and hand them out at the end of our meeting.

Following the speech, the leader invites everyone to take a few moments to introduce themselves. When everyone has had a turn, go around the circle again, having everyone introduce themselves as a fictional being.

The leader then introduces the Jumpstart exercise of her choice (see page 13), and the group begins to write. The leader is responsible for saying when it's time to wrap up each part of the process and in which direction the reading aloud should proceed.

The leader introduces a Postcard exercise (page 49), and the group proceeds to write and read aloud.

Ten minutes of free-writing is followed by a ten-minute break (see "Free-writing," page xiv).

The second half begins with a longer writing exercise, possibly "Our Bliss" (see page 103).

The leader then introduces Circle Writing, and the group creates Fairy Tales.

With ten minutes remaining, two rounds of "In the Manner of the Adverb" are played (see "Word Games," page 208), then the next week's leader and location are determined.

Two members have to leave, but five members hang out and socialize over tea and cookies.

DIRECTED SKETCHING

Directed Sketching is a wonderful variation on our basic Sketching exercise (page 30). When your group has become familiar with that basic exercise, choose a member to act as director. Her job is to call out an evocative word every five seconds or so while the other group members "sketch" the model. The words the sketchers write will spring from a combination of what they see *and* hear.

Here are three lists of words your director can use to direct the sketching.

LIST A	LIST B	LIST C
1. color	1. speed	1. energy
2. fruit	2. place	2. style
3. emotion	3. dance	3. music
4. animal	4. time	4. season
5. cloud	5. light	5. texture
6. flower	6. rhythm	6. tone
7. nation	7. weather	7. child

In an interesting variation on *this* variation, the director calls out words that come to her as she looks at the model. If you are the director, the key is to say whatever word comes into your mind without worrying about whether or not it obviously relates to the model.

Great

Minds

Think

Alike

Directed Sketching often produces a remarkable synchronicity of thought. At the first meeting of a group of writers who knew little or nothing about each other, I directed their sketching of one of the women. Among the words I called out was *animal.* To our collective astonishment, five of the six writers wrote the word *gazelle.* And this from a model sitting still!

As if this weren't amazing enough, on that same evening another model evoked the word *guitar* from all but one of the writers when I called out the word *music.* Unbeknownst to the other writers, the model was, indeed, a guitarist. Years later, in fact, he would open a guitar store.↩TW

For other group Sketching ideas, see the basic exercise on page 30.

Word Games

One writing group I belonged to liked to make every fifth meeting a game night. Shoeless, in comfortable clothes, we would play noncompetitive "Charades" and stage mock press conferences featuring one of us as a sudden celebrity. We would act out our dreams, the dreamer casting and directing the other members. We would play "In the Manner of the Adverb" and "What Are We?" Your group may eventually invent its own games. Meanwhile, here are two to get you started.

In the Manner of the Adverb

This game is great for breaking the ice and loosening up everyone's verbal faculties. After a game or two, it will be clear that the adverb chosen should be one that takes the guesser a little while to guess. It should also be one the group will enjoy acting out.

1. A member of the group leaves the room, going out of earshot.

2. The remaining members decide among themselves on an adverb. A simple choice would be *slowly.*

3. The person who left the room is summoned. He then asks a member of the group to do or say something in the manner of the adverb.

4. As the member attempts to do what she has been asked to do in the manner of the adverb (i.e. *slowly*), the person who left the room tries to guess what the adverb is.

Here are some things the guesser might ask a member or members to do in the manner of the adverb.

- "Introduce yourself to me."

- "Introduce yourself to another member of the group."

- "Sing a song."

- "Scratch your head."

- "Describe a sunset."

- "Look for something you've lost."

Some ideas for what he might ask the *whole* group to do in the manner of the adverb are:

- "Pretend you're having a party."

- "Pretend you're children playing together (unless you *are* children, then pretend to be adults having a business meeting)."

- "Pretend you've just been shipwrecked on an island."

- "Sing a song."

- "Dance."

VARIATION 1: To prolong the game, limit the guesser to three guesses for each requested enactment.

Variation 2: Have two people leave the room together. While waiting to be summoned, they can devise interesting ways for the group to enact the adverb.

What Are We?

Part of the challenge of "What Are We?" is in quickly designing *how* you and your cohorts are going to act out whatever you decide to be without making the answer too obvious. For instance, when we decided to be a blender making a fruit smoothie, three of us lay on the floor head-to head, flailing our legs around in the air, while the others became pieces of fruit bouncing off the flailers, dancing away and then dancing back.

Remember not to say or do anything so obvious that it gives away what you are. For instance, when we were members of The Secret Society of Thumb Suckers, we only sucked our thumbs when the person trying to guess wasn't looking directly at us. When we spoke about our society, we never mentioned thumb-sucking directly.

Basic Exercise	

1. A member of the group leaves the room, going out of earshot.

2. The remaining members decide among themselves what they collectively want to pretend to be. The possibilities are limitless. Here are some of the things we've come up with after years of playing this game.

   - a day-care center (teachers, students, parents)

   - compulsive worriers climbing Mount Everest

   - talking earthworms

   - logs going through a lumber mill

   - a baseball team in the dugout

   - a meeting of talking grocery store items

3. The person (or team) who left the room is summoned and tries to guess what the group is. If after several attempts the person doesn't guess correctly, the performers should

shift their behavior and/or provide more explicit verbal clues to make what they are more obvious.

4. If you are the person trying to guess, we recommend you let the group play at being what they are for a minute or two before making your first guess. A big part of the fun is in the enactment of the group creation.

$\mathcal{I}$DEAS FOR THE CLASSROOM

by Todd Walton

Teaching is not a lost art, but the regard for it is a lost tradition.
—JACQUES BARZUN

Dear Teacher,

      Over the past twenty years, I've been invited by your peers—in both private and public schools, at colleges and in prisons—to come to their classrooms for an hour, a day, or a week to introduce students to the writing exercises included in this volume. I have now had the honor of working with every age group from kindergarten through college and beyond, and I'm happy to say these exercises work well for all of them.

      As a result of my classroom experiences, my admiration for teachers has grown enormously. The amount of focused, positive energy required of a classroom teacher under the best of circumstances is simply phenomenal. That many teachers work in poorly supplied, over-crowded schools is one of the great failings of our society. I hope the information and ideas in this book, and particularly in this chapter, will be of some help to you.

ADAPTING EXERCISES
FROM THIS BOOK

Most of the exercises in this volume can be used in the classroom just as they are, but feel free to simplify or modify them
to fit the needs of a particular age group or individual student.
Each exercise was designed to illuminate a particular aspect of
the writing process. Students who do these exercises, whether
or not they produce any *finished* work, will be better prepared
for *all* the writing required of them in their lives.

Individual Work

Students can work on many of these exercises individually, in
class, or as homework assignments. Because the exercises are
designed primarily to engender a love of the writing process, I
recommend that if grades are to be given for this work, they be
based primarily on effort.

Partner and Circle Writing

Partner Writing (page 25), a two-person process, and Circle
Writing (page 28), a process for three or more people, are great
ways to harness the powerful socializing drive most students
possess. If you form writing circles within your class, try to
limit each circle to six students. Doing Circle Writing with
more than seven participants (of any age) tends to diminish the
effectiveness of the process.

I suggest that you experiment with same-gender and
mixed-gender partnering and circles. See which groupings
work best for your students. I highly recommend that dyads
and groups *not* be broken into "smart student" and "slow student" arrangements. Both Circle Writing and Partner Writing
can be effective, inspiring ways to intermingle disparate talents
and life experiences.

Writing partnerships can be used in a variety of ways. Random partnering and partnering by teacher design both work
well for writing exercises done in class. For out-of-class writing
projects, allowing students to choose their own homework

partners is a good way to harness friendship energy for the sake of writing practice.

Illustrations

There are probably several students in your class who like to draw. Encouraging students to add illustrations to their writing projects can make the assignments more appealing. For those who are self-conscious about drawing, "found" visuals or collages make excellent illustrations for stories or collections of poems.

Music

Some of the most sublime student writing I've ever heard came from free-writing to instrumental music. I highly recommend that you play evocative, meditative music during free-writing periods (see "Free-writing," page xiv).

BLACKBOARD EXERCISES

The Evolving Sentence

This process is a great way to begin a session of writing practice with your class. It illustrates the benefits of rewriting while encouraging expansive thinking. And if some or all of your students don't know what constitutes a verb, a noun, or an adjective, this is a quick, enjoyable way for them to learn the basic parts of speech.

Be aware that this exercise can unleash outbursts of "grossness" from students of all ages. I find that incorporating a few "gross" suggestions keeps the process fun and inclusive.

Caution: Some of these blackboard processes encourage students to call out words and ideas without raising their hands. This runs contrary to standard classroom etiquette and has proved annoying to some teachers. However, if you make it clear that hand-raising is being suspended only for a particular exercise, it's usually easy to restore order.

1. Ask the class to call out simple descriptive sentences. Select one and write it large on the blackboard. (You may also start this process by writing a simple sentence of your own invention.)

   A boy walked into the store.

> *Basic Process*

Technique Suggestions:

- This process is most effective when it goes fairly fast.
- As the students call out suggestions, select words that strike you as interesting or atypical.
- If there are students who want to be involved in the process but are shy about calling out a word, you might try saying, "Daniel, got an idea for another verb here?" If he doesn't respond quickly, take a suggestion from someone else.
- Try to do this process at least twice in a single session. Students who held back the first time are often emboldened to participate once they see that the process is purely fun.

2. Erase one of the words.

    A boy   into the store.

3. Say to the class, "Give me another verb here."

4. Several students may call out suggestions. Quickly choose one of their verbs and write it in place of the erased verb.

    A boy crashed into the store.

5. Erase another word.

    A boy crashed into the   .

6. Ask for a new noun.

    A boy crashed into the water.

7. Continue erasing and replacing words in this way. You may also expand the sentence by saying, "Give me an adjective for this noun." Then write the suggested word into the sentence.

    A gangly boy crashed into the water.

8. End the process when you feel you've gotten all you can out of the sentence. Leave the final sentence on the blackboard for your students to admire.

    Seven gnarly turtles vaporized the sickening toad.

9. Remind your students of the sentence you began with by writing it below the final sentence.

    A boy walked into the store.

Here are two suggestions for using the evolved sentences, either in class or as a homework assignment.

1. Write a short story that begins with one of the sentences you created together.

2. Using the Evolving Sentence process, create a first sentence and a last sentence. Have everyone write a short story that connects the two sentences.

Creation of Writing Vocabulary

This process encourages the expansion of vocabulary while giving your students a sense of participation in the design of their writing exercises. Try for a balance of nouns, verbs, and modifiers.

1. Ask the class to suggest words they'd like to use in a warm-up exercise.

Basic Process

2. When you've written down a dozen words, ask for definitions. When all the words have been correctly defined, describe the writing assignment that will incorporate these words. Here are some writing exercises your students can do using student-generated vocabulary.

   Note: You may want to limit the number of popular slang words, but include a few if they come up.

   - Use all the words correctly in a single paragraph.

   - Use all the words in a short story.

   - Use all the words in a poem.

   - Use all the words in a letter to the teacher (you).

   - Use all the words in a dialogue between two characters.

Stories from Visuals

1 Ask for a volunteer to draw a large picture on the blackboard.

Basic Process

2. While she is drawing her picture, ask the other students to close their eyes and relax. Tell them they are going to be writing a poem or a story inspired by the picture they see on the blackboard when they open their eyes.

   Note: Please read the section on Stories From Visuals (page 160) before trying this blackboard exercise.

3. Once the drawing is done, allow your students fifteen to twenty minutes to write as much as they can. Make it clear that they don't have to finish their poems or stories. If they *do* finish a first draft before time is up, have them do some refining of their work.

VARIATION 1: Have several students draw pictures so the class has a sequence of images to inspire their creations.

Variation 2: Ask three of your students to form some sort of tableau—a group pose—in front of the class, then have the other students write a poem or story inspired by this scene.

Creating Arbitrary Story Structures

<table>
<tr>
<td>

Basic Process

</td>
<td>

1. After you have a good understanding of how Arbitrary Story Structures work, explain the concept to your students.

2. Ask the class to suggest the first part of a story. Number and write this first part on the blackboard. For example:

Part 1. Someone is somewhere.

2. Ask for another part. Number and write this suggestion below the first one. For example:

Part 2. They remember something important.

</td>
</tr>
</table>

Notes:
- Please read the section on Arbitrary Story Structures (page 148) before undertaking this blackboard exercise.
- You may want to reinstate the raising of hands for this exercise. You might also limit suggestions to one per student.

3. Repeat this process until you have a seven-part structure.

4. Ask your students to each write a story following this Arbitrary Story Structure, or break the class into partners and have them create their stories using Partner Writing (see page 25). You may also break the class into small groups to create their stories using Circle Writing (page 28).

Variation 1: Once the story structure is written on the blackboard, use the same erasing and replacing method described in "The Evolving Sentence" (page 217) to take the story structure through a spontaneous evolution. Use the final structure for individual or group writing processes.

Biography Data Sheets

<table>
<tr>
<td>

Basic Process

</td>
<td>

1. Copy the Biography Data Sheet (page 101) onto the blackboard (or blackboards), leaving space between the categories to write in data.

2. Explain the purpose of Biography Data Sheets.

3. Elicit data from the class. I use two different methods for doing this. The more chaotic (but often more enjoyable) method is to have your students call out suggestions for each data category, while you make the choices from the

</td>
</tr>
</table>

various suggestions you hear. The other method (probably more inclusive) is to call on students one-by-one to supply the data for the various categories. You may allow your students to choose the unfilled categories for which they want to supply data, or have them supply data in the order in which the categories appear.

Note: Please read the section on "Biography Data Sheets" (page 100) before undertaking this blackboard exercise.

4. When the data sheet is filled out, read the data aloud.

5. Ask the class if there is anything they'd like to change about the character they've created. If so, why? Anything they wish to add? Why? This is a good way to start a discussion about characters, stereotypes, and where we get our ideas.

A Fantastic Class Project

There is a marvelous way to combine a class-generated Arbitrary Story Structure and a class-generated Biography Data Sheet to give your students the experience of writing a novella. This process can be done in one day or over the course of a few days, depending on how polished you want the final creation to be.

1. Using the technique described in "Inventing Your Own Structures" (page 154), create an arbitrary structure with as many steps as there are students in your class. Each student will suggest one of the parts. Write down these parts, in order, on the blackboard. If you have fewer than fifteen students in your class, have each student suggest two parts.

Basic Process

2. Each student copies the parts down on a piece of paper.

3. Using the technique described above for Biography Data Sheets, fill out a Biography Data Sheet on the blackboard.

4. When you and your students are satisfied with the character you've created, each student copies this information onto a blank Biography Data Sheet.

5. Assign the writing of one part of the story structure to each student, using the class-created character as the protagonist.

6. Each student writes a draft—one to two pages long—for her chapter of the story.

7. Students read their chapters aloud, in the order of the Arbitrary Structure. This completes the basic process.

Depending on the interest and sophistication of your class, you may add the following steps:

8. Divide the class into groups of five students who have written consecutive chapters: 1–5, 6–10, 11–15, 16–20, and so on. The groups share their rough drafts among themselves, then work as a team to modify their beginnings and endings so the parts flow together more meaningfully.

9. When the transitions between chapters are complete, the writers reconsider their individual chapters and make whatever changes they see fit.

10. Those students with linked parts who have not yet conferred—5 and 6, 10 and 11, 15 and 16, and so on—meet separately to craft new beginnings and endings so their parts flow together.

11. The entire opus is assembled and read aloud by students who volunteer to read.

PERFORMANCE

I'm a big proponent of *not* insisting a student read aloud in front of the class if he or she doesn't want to. Voluntary performance is much more relaxed and enjoyable than mandatory performance. A voluntary performance policy invariably leads—over time—to most students sharing their work.

If there are students who never volunteer to read, I believe in honoring that choice. When a student knows her creative writing is private until she chooses to share it, she will write with greater freedom, imagination, and emotion.

In every class I have taught, at least one student has been

willing and eager to read other students' work aloud. By permitting reluctant students to choose someone else (including you) to read their stories or poems to the class, you create a transitional experience that emboldens those students to read their own work. When a student hears her work read aloud and it is received without criticism, the experience can be life-changing.

I am forever astonished and heartened by the support students offer each other when their works are read out loud. This generous and loving support tends to fade somewhat in college settings. But even there, once students become accustomed to a writing process free of judgment and comparison, support for the work of others is nearly universal. Such peer support, I feel, is an invaluable encouragement for a student to continue on the writer's path.

Writers and Actors

If you work in a school where one class is permitted to visit another, joint projects between writers and actors are a fantastic means of stimulating inter-disciplinary creativity. Asking your writing students to create monologues, scenes, short stories, and poems for acting students to perform is great fun and tremendously empowering for writers and actors alike. Partner Writing is a particularly effective technique for creating performable scenes. The more theatrical the setting for the performance, the better.

Even if you can't arrange to work with other classes, writing and performing scenes in class is a terrific way to get students to work together. Some students will just want to act, some will just want to write, and some will want to do both.

Note: Offering scene-writing as an optional homework assignment can be just the spark some of your students need to become more engaged in writing.

MAKING BOOKS

Making books of our writing can be a deeply empowering experience for writers of any age. The very idea that their poems or stories or essays will be made into a book inspires enormous enthusiasm in young writers. Books can be made in an hour or over the course of several months, by individuals, partners, or groups. Here are two book-making processes that have worked well for me.

A Book of Illustrated Poems

1. Give each student one week to collect seven images they love—photographs, postcards, magazine clippings, and the like.

2. Instruct them to assemble the images in an order they like.

3. Ask them to write a short poem inspired by each of the images, then to rewrite the poems if they wish.

4. Have them copy the poems as neatly as they can on sheets of unlined paper, one poem per sheet.

5. Show them how to assemble their poems and corresponding images so that each poem is situated on the page facing the image that inspired it.

6. Ask them to title their collection and create a cover.

7. Show them what a dedication page looks like and ask them to dedicate their volume to someone.

8. Demonstrate how to carefully staple the sides of the volume together so it opens like a real book.

VARIATION 1: If your students have access to a copy machine or computer, they can make several copies to distribute among family and friends, if they wish.

VARIATION 2: To make their books more special, students may use a sturdier cover stock and sew their books together.

A Book of Letters

Basic Process

1. Divide the class into pairs, by teacher design or student choice.

2. Have each pair of students flip a coin to determine who will write the first letter.

3. Have the two students exchange addresses.

4. On the first day of this process, a first letter is written, placed in an envelope, addressed, stamped, and given to the teacher to be mailed.

5. Instruct students to make it a homework priority to answer the letters they receive and mail their responses as soon as possible, preferably on the day they receive each letter.

6. After two weeks, each student should have received several letters. Have the writing partners assemble their letters into a single volume, edit and illustrate it however they wish, then make at least two neat copies of the opus to be bound.

VARIATION 1: A specific topic may be chosen or assigned as a focus for the letters.

VARIATION 2: The exchange may be assigned as a fiction-writing project, with the letters as alternating chapters.

VARIATION 3: Your students may assume fictional identities for the purpose of the letter exchange.

CREATION OF CLANS

The creation of clans is one of the most successful group writing exercises I've ever done with teenagers, but it also works well for younger and older writers. The process requires that each clan be able to convene out of sight and earshot of the other clans. Allow two hours for the clans to prepare their presentations.

1. Divide the class or group into clans of six to eight writers each. You may do this randomly, by teacher design, or by student choice.

2. Give each clan a copy or copies of the following checklist, or some variation created by you.

Basic Process

CLAN CREATION CHECKLIST

- What is the name of your clan?

- What are your individual names within the clan?

- What is your system of governance?

- How do you make decisions?

- Who or what do you worship? How?

- What is the moral code of your clan—the ten (or so) commandments?

- What is your sacred food? How is it prepared?

- Create—and be prepared to read, recite, or chant— your clan creation myth.

- Who are your enemies? How do you relate to them?

- Who are your allies? How do you relate to them?

- Create, and be prepared to perform, your clan song and dance.

- Design and rehearse a comprehensive presentation of the above clan attributes to be performed in front of the great assembly of clans.

3. Assemble the clans in the most theatrical setting possible.

4. Draw numbers to determine the order in which the clans will perform.

5. Have fun!

INTERVIEWS

TEACHER: What about the interview process? How can I adapt that to classroom use?

TW: Great question. My experience has been that kids, particularly teenagers, love to interview each other. For partner writing, the interview is a great way to generate material for autobiographies, personal essays, and fiction. For the whole class, staging a press conference can be both entertaining and illuminating. Also, you might consider having your students interview *you* about the subject you're teaching or about life in general.

TEACHER: To sharpen their investigative skills?

TW: Yes, and to give you a sense of what they find intriguing about a subject.

TEACHER: Any other suggestions?

TW: Stage a talk show. Have one student be the host, have two other students be the producers. They invite three or four students to come on the show, and in the days preceding the show they collaborate on creating the questions the host will ask.

TEACHER: Sounds ambitious.

TW: It can be as simple or as elaborate as you and your students decide to make it.

Acknowledgments

Hats off to the irrepressible Helen Gustafson for opening the door to Phil Wood, who instantly recognized *The Writer's Path* as "just the thing" for Ten Speed Press. The production team he put in place was outstanding. Dave Peattie was a peach of a project manager, overseeing the impeccable copyediting of Kristi Hein, the keen eye of Katherine Silver, and the splendid design work of Tasha Hall and Catherine Jacobes.

Bill Yates and Carolyn Schneider, friends and fellow artists, added their wit and poetry to the Circle Writing examples.

Enormous thanks to our many friends and mentors who have uplifted and inspired us by following their hearts along the creative path.

Todd Walton lives in Berkeley, California, where he writes stories, essays, and poetry. He also composes music and is an accomplished gardener. His published novels are *Inside Moves, Forgotten Impulses, Louise & Women, Night Train,* and *Ruby & Spear.* His chapbook, *Of Water and Melons,* and his first nonfiction book, *Open Body: Creating Your Own Yoga,* were both illustrated by Vance Lawry.

Mindy Toomay is a writer, editor, and cook who plies the literary and culinary trades in Berkeley, California. Her eleven published books include *The Vegan Gourmet* (with Susann Geiskopf-Hadler) and *A Cozy Book of Herbal Teas: Recipes, Remedies, and Folk Wisdom.*

Index